me,
you
&
the
kids
too

me, you & the kids too

Renée Elliott

DUNCAN BAIRD PUBLISHERS

LONDON

ME, YOU & THE KIDS TOO
Renée Elliott

First published in the United Kingdom and Ireland in 2012
by Duncan Baird Publishers Ltd
Sixth Floor, Castle House, 75–76 Wells Street
London W1T 3QH

Conceived, created and designed by Duncan Baird Publishers

Managing Editor: Grace Cheetham
Editors: Nicole Bator, Gillian Haslam and Krissy Mallett
Managing Designer: Manisha Patel
Design: Blok Graphic
Production: Uzma Taj
Commissioned Photography: Dan Jones
Artwork: Jessica Elliott and Nicholas Elliott
Food Stylists: Bianca Nice and Sue Henderson
Prop Stylist: Sue Rowlands

British Library Cataloguing-in-Publication Data:
A CIP record for this book is available from the British Library

ISBN: 978-1-84899-006-7

10 9 8 7 6 5 4 3 2 1

Typeset in Scala Sans and ITC American Typewriter
Colour reproduction by Colourscan
Printed in Singapore by Imago

Publisher's note

*To my mom, Lucille, and my dad, Edward. And also
to Grace, my editor, who gave this book so much.*

Vegetarian recipes
Vegetarian recipes in this book contain no meat, poultry,
game, fish or shellfish. They may include eggs or cheese.
Cheese, especially those made using traditional methods,
may contain calf rennet, so check labels first. Look for
'suitable for vegetarians', the 'V' sign or 'contains
vegetarian rennet' on the label.

Unless otherwise stated:
- All recipes serve 2 adults, 1 child and 1 baby
- Preparation and cooking times refer to the main
  recipes only
- Use organic ingredients
- Use wild salmon
- Use large eggs
- Use medium fruit and vegetables
- Use fresh ingredients, including herbs
- Do not mix metric and imperial measurements
- 1 tsp = 5ml   1 tbsp = 15ml   1 cup = 250ml

Acknowledgments

The biggest thanks must go to my husband Brian. He is
my rock. He ate all of the food and took care of the children.
Thanks to my kids Jess, Nicholas and Cassie who wanted me
to be with them all of the time, but let me work. And thanks
to Jess and Nicholas who were part of the photography and
drew the pictures that are in the book.

There would not be a book – or it would not be so perfect
– without Grace, Krissy, Nicole, Gillian, Manisha and Allan.
A huge thank you to Borra for always listening, and for her
support and encouragement.

And a sweet thank you to Niamh, Zoë and Josie who
were also photographed.

I wanted this book to be triple tested – and not just by
me. There is a huge and heartfelt thank you for the recipe
testers who cooked and baked for me – my mother, Lucille,
my brother, David, and my sisters, Jan and Lauren. And thank
you to my friends, Allison, Annabel, Jazz, Julia, Julie, Kate
and Simon. They cooked my creations for themselves, their
children, their builders – and their friends. And everyone
came back with ideas and suggestions and comments that
helped shape this book into something much better than it
was. Like any journey, it's better travelled in the company
of family and friends.

Contents

Introduction

A friend once said to me that raising kids is simple – all you have to do is marinate them in love for 18 years and then send them out into the world. I agree with this completely and from my perspective, the second priority – if you want them to be strong, live well and fulfil their potential – is to feed them nutritious food so that they have good health. Without wellbeing, it is difficult or impossible to do anything. Yet with a foundation of health and vitality, your children can pursue their dreams.

Before I had my eldest daughter, Jessica, I was a pretty good cook. I had been working in natural foods for ten years and cared about what I ate. I made home-cooked food and liked to bake occasionally. When Jessie was born, I happily breast-fed her for four months, but when she started to reach for my spoon, I realized that I actually had no idea how or what to cook for a baby. I hadn't planned on giving her jarred baby food because I knew instinctively that I wanted

to give her fresh, home-made meals. But, other than that, I didn't know what to do.

I knew I didn't want her to have refined foods, like white rice and white flour, because they are so low in nutrition, and I wondered whether she should be eating things like gluten, dairy or soya early on. I found one great book, did lots of nutritional research and quizzed many experts – and formulated a feeding plan as I went. I took notes on recipes I created and techniques I discovered and carried on in the same way when I had my second child, Nicholas. My babies flourished and when my youngest, Cassandra, was ready to wean, I wrote it all down in my first book, *The Best Recipes for Babies & Toddlers*.

However, with work and three young children, I was so tired and busy, that cooking for myself and my husband, Brian, was too often an afterthought. I knew that I had to be well nourished in order to be able to take care of everyone else, but I would make gorgeous meals for them and then wonder what on earth we were going to eat. And I was often too befuddled from the broken nights to figure it out.

My editor, Grace, who had a young baby, was going through the same experience. She said, 'What we need is a book for the whole family – a book that helps people cook great meals for themselves, as well as their kids, so they can take care of their needs at the same time as providing the best start for their baby.' And so this book was born.

This book is filled with the most nourishing and delicious meals for you and your family. Just pick a recipe and, from that recipe, comes food for you, your partner and your kids – as well as a step-by-step guide to preparing a meal for your baby at the same time. You don't need extra ingredients and it's all worked out for you – whether you have a 6–9 or 9–12 month old.

Like all parents, I don't always do a perfect job. But I have managed to incorporate some solid nutritional basics into our daily and weekly routines, such as using wholemeal flours, eating different grains and including superfoods such as seaweeds and seeds. You'll never

begin all of them at once, so just take it slowly. But I hope that you will be inspired to pick some things out of the book that spark your interest and gradually try to make each one a habit – like changing your baking to use wholemeal spelt flour or not buying sweetened breakfast cereals.

When you decide you want a baby and imagine lying on the sofa snuggling your little one, the last thing on your mind is the amount of cooking you will be doing for that little person. But even if cooking isn't really your thing – or hasn't been up until now – it's a fact of life that if you want to make nourishing food, then someone needs to get in the kitchen!

There is a lot of food to prepare for kids who can't do anything for themselves in the kitchen for many years. I realized that I needed to work out a way to make my family's meals easily – without having to take time from all of the other things I needed to do (like working and getting some sleep myself).

However, this book isn't just about cooking for your baby and kids; it's about cooking great meals for you and your partner, too. You'll find it easy to cook something delicious for yourselves and enjoy some

time together in the evening, all the while making sure you're nourishing yourself.

Although some of these recipes may take time on the hob or in the oven, they are all very simple to make – using quick preparation techniques and very easy steps to follow. And while you're cooking the meal, you can whizz up a meal for your baby, too. You don't have to puzzle anything out, and the recipes make cooking for your baby a breeze because you're using the same ingredients for your meal.

How this book works

This book is for feeding the whole family and, unless otherwise stated, the recipes are for two adults, one young child and one baby. You can choose a recipe and cook it for you and your family. Simply make a little more of the recipe if you're feeding more than one child and if you're cooking for just you and your partner, you'll have leftovers for the following day – or for your freezer. If you want to cook for a 6–9 month old or a 9–12 month old, simply make it when you make the main meal.

As you follow the method for the main recipe, you will see signs showing 6-9 or 9-12 – these tell you when you need to set aside some of the ingredients or mixture for your baby. Then go to the corresponding method for either age group and follow that method to make the extra meal. Because the types of foods that your baby can eat increase at every stage of development, the recipes for the 9–12 month old build on the recipes for the 6–9 month old. When your baby is a year old, you can use the main recipe.

For 6–9 months, you need a good selection of purées made from the foods listed in the chart on page 20. From 9–12 months you can include more foods and you can either make a lumpy purée or try some small pieces of food. From 12 months onwards, your child can eat what you eat – although you may want to go easy on spices and strong flavours, and continue to avoid salt.

I have made all the recipes as simple as possible. When I read recipes that want me to steam or sauté vegetables beforehand or have lots of separate fiddly steps, I assume they are not aimed at someone with a baby. When you are a parent, you need things to be really simple and easy because you have so much else going on. So, for example, before I make the quiche, I don't steam the broccoli as it will cook in the oven, and I don't sauté the onions. The flavours are still great – and the whole recipe is incredibly quick to make.

Don't be put off trying a recipe that has an ingredient you are not familiar with. In the ingredients list, it may say yogurt or kefir, wholemeal spelt flour or wholemeal plain flour, so buy what is easier for you. After you have tried a recipe, like it and want to make it again, then try the more unusual ingredient. My goal is to introduce you gradually to different and better foods and expand your palate and repertoire of ingredients.

Also, don't worry about buying unusual ingredients like kuzu and quinoa, which you think you won't use up. There are enough recipes in the book to use these great ingredients. Don't be afraid to buy something that you've never used before or don't know if you will like. If you make one dish that isn't your favourite, the index can help you find other recipes using specific ingredients.

I love making my own beans but you may not have the time, so buy tinned ones instead. Don't worry – it's something you can choose to do in the future. What I'm saying is don't *not* try a recipe because of that. You've got to make your life easy. I am showing you the most nutritious way to prepare food, but it has to work in your life at the time.

Why healthy?

Without doubt, what your baby eats affects his or her health today and in the future. If your child starts off eating a narrow range of foods, he or she is likely to continue doing so throughout his or her life – and may not get a complete spectrum of nutrients. This can impact on his or her health both in the formative years and also later in life.

Eating a wide range of foods creates a strong foundation of health and increases your chance of getting the necessary nutrients. It creates adventurous eating in your children as they grow, and if they ever get finicky about what they eat, they will still have a wide range of foods to choose from. You can get children used to healthy tastes from an early age and this will nourish them for rest of their lives. Even if your child rebels against your cooking and wholemeal bread at some point, the likelihood is that he or she will come back to what he or she knows – and the tastes that are familiar … eventually.

So think about shaping your children's palates to love foods such as unsweetened yogurt, unsweetened porridge, wholemeal pasta, sourdough rye, sprouts, nuts and seeds. And because treats like chocolate are probably inevitable, and so delectable, you don't have to forbid them – but choose the best, which is dark, organic chocolate.

Why organic?

There's a question. Yes, yes, there are so many labels out there. How could you possibly choose? Well, it's really quite simple. If you want the best-quality food, choose organic. If you want meat and dairy products that don't carry antibiotic residues; if you want fruit and vegetables without pesticide residues; if you want to eat food that is free from genetically modified ingredients; and if you don't want to have to examine food labels to ensure the food doesn't contain any nasty additives, choose organic.

If you find it difficult to find everything organically or if it's too expensive, start with what you eat the most of, and also opt for organic fruit and vegetables. If you can buy organic dairy products, which are higher in essential fatty acids and other essential nutrients, that's an added bonus. Organic meat is expensive to farm and therefore costs more. So rather than spend more on meat, you can buy less of it and eat better quality.

What is healthy food?

Healthy food is everything that nature hands directly to us – seeds, nuts, beans, vegetables, fruits, grains, fish and meat. When you cook at home using these ingredients, the meals you make will nourish and sustain you.

The most basic advice for healthy eating is this: avoid highly-processed foods, sweets, fried foods, junk food, fizzy drinks, white flour, sugar, salt and cheap fats. Instead, fill yourselves with natural ingredients that are full of nutrients. If you can eat a rainbow of foods every day – a whole range of different-coloured foods – you'll be doing well. And if you can add superfoods in, too, you'll be doing brilliantly. Try the recipes – and try the superfood ingredients, even if you've never heard of them and have to order them from a health food shop. I've worked out easy ways to incorporate them into your recipes – and into your life.

Healthy food for the whole family

What do I feed my baby?

When a baby is born, he or she is ready only for mother's milk. At any time after 4 months, a baby may want solid foods. There is much debate about how long you should breast feed and at what age you should introduce solids, but I think if you pay attention to your child and listen to your intuition, you will know when the time is right. My first daughter, Jessica, who was very little when she was born, couldn't take her eyes off my fork when she was 4 months old so I weaned her then. Whatever you do, the most important thing is to start very, very gently.

For the first two years, a baby's digestive and immune systems are not fully developed. For this reason, it makes sense to introduce foods carefully. That is why I wait to introduce certain foods until they have developed a little more. For example, I don't introduce dairy (other than yogurt for soaking) until 9–12 months and I leave introducing gluten, foods in the deadly nightshade family (tomatoes, aubergine, potatoes and so on) and yeasty foods such as mushrooms until 1 year. Many of these foods are either harder to digest or are associated with allergies. We may not know for a very long time – if ever – what the perfect foods are for a baby to eat at each stage, but this approach is thoughtful and mindful of the limitations of an immature and developing body. If you want to avoid cow's milk, your baby can get great calcium at different stages from yogurt, cheese, dark green vegetables (broccoli, kale, spinach, turnip greens and spring greens), oranges, tempeh, peas, black beans, sardines, sesame seeds and almonds.

Meals for everyone

It's important that each day everyone in the family has a good balance of protein, carbohydrates, vegetables and fat. There is protein in meats, fish, dairy products, eggs, beans, wholemeal grains, vegetables, nuts and seeds. This book provides healthy meals for everyone – from parents or carers to toddlers and the baby who's just starting to enjoy food. Good health comes from the ingredients, the wholeness and the way you cook them – for example, if you soak and steam. If you eat like this some or most of the time, you'll be doing really well.

All you hear about these days is to avoid sugar, salt and fat. Well, it's more complicated than that and I don't think you can say 'don't do this' and then not talk about the better alternatives. That's what this section is about. And it's about moderation.

Sugar

I'm not crazy about sugar. I love the taste of it, but I hate what it does to the body, especially over a long period of time. It creates stress by forcing your body to adjust to the high blood sugar levels it creates. If this stress continues over a long period, it can lead to Type 2 diabetes. Furthermore, too much sugar in your body gets converted to fat.

I see two huge problems around sugar. One is having desserts every day or after every meal, which can lead to a terrible lifelong habit. And the other is that sugar isn't just found in sweet things – it's also in many savoury processed foods, too. Reduce the sugar that you eat, cut down on desserts and avoid giving it to your baby for as long as you possibly can.

Organic cane sugar is better than conventional white refined sugar because of the processing involved, but rice malt syrup and agave stand head and shoulders above all sweeteners. Rice malt syrup, a delicately flavoured natural sweetener, is made up mostly of complex sugars and therefore, unlike white sugar, releases slowly into the bloodstream.

Salt

There is bad salt and there is good salt. Much salt on the market is so over-refined that manufacturers add iodine back into it. Babies don't need it, but as children grow up, it's not the salt in your cooking that will be a problem, but the salt in snacks like crisps, junk food and processed meals, which are cheaply made and rely on salt for flavour. Use a good sea salt moderately in your cooking. I have specified amounts of salt in each recipe to give you guidelines on healthy quantities.

Fats

Fats are necessary and important in our diets. They provide energy, they are building blocks for cell membranes and hormones, they keep us full, carry fat-soluble vitamins and support many other body processes. However, there is good fat and bad fat. Play it smart. Don't buy anything that contains hydrogenated or partially-hydrogenated fat and reduce or eliminate the amount of fried foods you eat.

But do enjoy cold-pressed seed oils to get the essential good fats that your body needs every day. Don't worry about eating fat in dairy products and in good-quality meats. It's the fat that gives it the flavour (you often find low-fat yogurts have lots of added sugar to give them flavour) and babies need good fat. Buy butter, not margarine, and full-fat yogurt – and cut out cheap and greasy snack foods.

Milk

I firmly believe that cow's milk is meant for baby cows, not for human beings. Our digestive systems are not designed to process cow's milk and it can cause real health problems in many children and adults. You'll find that there are wonderful alternatives available – you can use rice milk, oat milk or water instead of milk. All the recipes in this book suggest these alternatives.

Meat

What's important is to eat quality, grass-fed meats. It makes sense to spend the same amount of money per week on meat, but buy organic, which is more expensive to produce but much better quality. In the food pyramid, remember that as well as meat, protein is found in poultry, fish, beans, eggs, nuts and seeds. Stay away from sausages, luncheon meats and other processed meats, which really aren't worth eating.

Whole grains

Whole grains are full of goodness. As well as vitamins and minerals, they also contain valuable protein. What's more, you can enhance their nutritional status. When our ancestors ate whole grains, they didn't eat quick-rise breads and hastily prepared porridge. They soaked or fermented grains first. And, of course, there is a good reason for this.

Soaking whole grains allows two important processes to take place. All grains contain phytic acid in the outer layer. In our bodies, the phytic acid binds with calcium, copper, iron, magnesium and zinc (for a strong immune system) and prevents us from absorbing them. Neutralizing the phytic acid is done simply by soaking the grain in warm acidulated water for at least seven hours. Soaking with a spoonful of yogurt allows enzymes like lactobacilli to break down and neutralize the phytic acid. The other beneficial reason is that soaking grains in warm water encourages them to produce their own enzymes, which then increases the quantity of B vitamins you will eat.

When a recipe says serve with rice or a grain, try the following variations:

RICE: black, brown basmati, jasmine, long grain, red Camargue, short grain, Thai and wild.

GRAINS: amaranth, barley, buckwheat, corn, Kamut, millet, oat, quinoa, rye, spelt and wheat.

FLAKES: barley, buckwheat, Kamut, millet, oats, quinoa, rice, rye, spelt and wheat.

FLOURS: barley, buckwheat, chestnut, chickpea, coconut, corn, Kamut, oat, rye, spelt and wheat.

Wholemeal flour

Nature has given us all of the goodness and fibre we need in a grain if we eat the whole thing, which is why you should eat wholemeal flour whenever possible.

There isn't a lot of point in eating white flour as manufacturers remove the two most nutritious and fibre-rich parts of the seed – the outside bran layer and the inside germ. It is so stripped of its goodness that synthetic vitamins are added back into it. To add insult to injury, white flour is then bleached. Your body can't tell the difference between white sugar and white flour.

White flour is the other sugar.

When someone eats refined carbohydrates (white flour, cereals, bread, biscuits, snacks) or simple sugars, they require very little metabolism by the body, so they enter the bloodstream rapidly. This causes a quick rise in blood sugar levels, which triggers a similarly rapid release of the body's sugar-regulating hormone, insulin. This gives you the 'lift' followed by the 'crash', which makes you feel tired and down. If this happens over a long period of time, it may lead to thrombosis, high blood pressure, heart disease, hypoglycemia, Type 2 diabetes, decreased immune function and adrenal stress. Try not to cook white rice or pasta at home. You can eat it sometimes, but have it when out at restaurants or friends' houses and eat the good stuff at home.

Adding nutrition

As food plays such a huge part in our health, I like to add extra nutrition wherever possible (this is especially important with children who may not be big eaters). That's why I like to use ingredients like kuzu and miso (see pages 15 and 16) instead of corn flour and salt. Also try serving a little nori at mealtime, sprinkling furikake (a mix of sesame seeds and seaweed) on your child's rice or pasta and adding sprouts in when you can. And give them healthy snacks between meals, such as tahini on rice crackers, fruit, vegetable sticks, unsweetened popcorn, nuts and seeds.

Helpful hints

If you want to make changes to the way you eat, don't try to do everything at once. If you do, the chances are that it won't be fun or enjoyable, you will become stressed and you'll go back to the way you were eating before. Try changing one thing a month or every few months. Make it simple, like switching to wholemeal bread or buying unsweetened organic yogurt. Eat some raw and cooked vegetables, of different colours, at every meal. Eat a rainbow of foods every day. Get your kids cooking with you as soon as they are interested. If you have older children, look at their favourite foods and make subtle, healthy changes. For example, if they love pizza, make it with wholemeal crust. If they eat salad, add seeds. Mix natural yogurt into home-made cereal, instead of highly-processed breakfast cereals.

Wonderfoods

Other than apple, avocado and broccoli, I'm not going to talk about most of the usual wonder- or superfoods. All fresh, organic foods as basic ingredients are quite wonderful and have something special about the nutrients they offer us. They are more wonderful when you eat them in season, because they are at their optimum in terms of growing and ripening. Most of the foods listed below are special because they offer something above and beyond what most people eat every day and are worth including in your diet.

Amaranth
Originally found in South America and Mexico, amaranth dates back about 8,000 years in the human diet. It is packed with nutrients and is 15–17% protein. Amaranth is vitamin rich and a good source of vitamins A, B6, C, folate and riboflavin. It has lots of minerals and is loaded with fibre. Amaranth benefits the immune system, helps with hypertension and cardiovascular disease. And it tastes good.

Apple
You've got to love apples! They are always available, easy to grow and store, inexpensive and truly and simply delicious. Not only that, but they also increase bone density, reduce wheezing from asthma, protect against lung, breast, colon and liver cancers and Alzheimer's, help with diabetes and can help you lose weight.

Avocado
Ah, one of my four favourite foods. Avocado is considered by many to be a perfect food because it is so good for you. It is absolutely wonderful for babies, providing them with fabulous fat and filling them up

with goodness. Avocado is the best fruit source of vitamin E, which is great for overall health. It is also good for your eyes, heart, skin, prostate, absorption of food nutrients, and helps to prevent different cancers of the mouth, skin and prostate because of its special mix of anti-inflammatory and antioxidant nutrients.

Cut in half, remove the stone and fill the hole with oil and vinegar. Add slices to sandwiches – especially good with hummus – or salads. Mash it into a dip or guacamole or whizz it into a smoothie.

Broccoli
Broccoli is part of the cruciferous family of vegetables, which are so good for you that they should be eaten at least three times a week. Steaming is the best way to eat broccoli because it retains its goodness, stays slightly crunchy and most kids really love it cooked that way. Don't overcook it to the point where it is dark and mushy. Broccoli helps metabolize vitamin D,

it helps the body detoxify and it lessens the effect of allergens in our bodies.

Buckwheat

Another great grain to add into your diet, buckwheat has a wonderful nutritional profile. One of its benefits is that it contains almost 86 milligrams of magnesium in 1 cup. Magnesium relaxes blood vessels, improves blood flow and therefore the delivery of nutrients throughout the body while reducing blood pressure. A complex carbohydrate, buckwheat is energizing whether you have it as porridge for breakfast or as part of your lunch or dinner.

Garlic

Garlic has two main beneficial effects on the body. The first is that it is a powerful and natural antibiotic and antifungal, and the second is that it is good for the immune system.

I used to think of garlic as a cooking condiment, but now I use it as a vegetable in its own right. I used to consider that three cloves of garlic was a lot, but now I always seem to use an entire head.

Kefir

Kefir is called a miracle food. It is made by culturing fresh milk, water and kefir grains, which are clumps of bacteria proven to be highly beneficial to our digestive system. Kefir is similar to yogurt in taste, but as well as containing healthy bacteria, kefir also contains healthy yeasts. Kefir enhances the micro-organisms of the intestines, which assist in digestion. It stimulates the immune system, protects against harmful bacteria and is packed with vitamins, minerals, amino acids and enzymes.

Kuzu

You probably use a thickening agent in some of your cooking, but instead of using cornflour, which has no nutritional value and is heavily bleached (unless organic), you could switch to kuzu, a starch made from the root of the kuzu or kudzu plant. Plants concentrate their energy in their roots, which is why root vegetables are so valuable to eat and why some roots, such as ginseng, are known for their medicinal qualities.

In Japan and China, kuzu is known for its excellence as a thickening and jelling agent and for its healing properties for digestive disorders, such as stomach aches and diarrhoea. Kuzu is full of flavonoids, which relax constricted blood vessels. This means it can help ease headaches, migraines and high blood pressure. Kuzu also neutralizes lactic acid and eliminates it from the body, and relaxes tight muscles.

Kuzu comes in chunks. Crush it into a powder with the back of a spoon and use about 1½ tablespoons of kuzu to each 240ml/8fl oz/scant 1 cup of liquid for sauces and gravies, and 2 tablespoons per 240ml/ 8fl oz/scant 1 cup of liquid for jelling.

Millet

A great and underused gluten-free grain, millet is highly nutritious and alkaline, easy to digest and soothing to the digestive system. It is called by some the most digestible and least allergenic grain in the world. Nearly 15% protein, millet is also high in fibre, B vitamins, vitamin E and important minerals. Great for porridge in the morning or instead of pasta or rice.

Miso

A fermented soya product, miso is delicious, useful and medicinal. You can use miso instead of salt in soups and bakes to add a richness of flavour. Miso is a good source of amino acids and is like yogurt in that it is full of lactic-acid bacteria and enzymes that aid digestion. Recent scientific research shows that miso helps the body get rid of some carcinogens, acidity, radiation and the effects of smoking and pollution.

At the end of cooking, take some of the broth from the soup or stew, dissolve a tablespoon or so of miso in it, then stir it back in. It may be briefly simmered, but boiling miso will destroy its health-giving properties.

Nuts

Nuts are one of the best plant sources of protein. They are high in good fats and rich in fibre, phytonutrients and antioxidants. Almonds are particularly fabulous and I always have a bowl of them out for the kids to snack on. Almonds help to regulate blood pressure, prevent cancer, protect against diabetes, boost your energy, reduce risk of heart disease, improve brain power and prevent birth defects. Peanuts, however, should wait until your child is 5 years old.

Oils

Your body needs essential fatty acids every day, because it can't manufacture them from other things you eat. Cold-pressed seed oils are an excellent source of essential fats. Choose from flax, hemp, pumpkin, safflower, sesame and sunflower. Hemp is the best oil, but any of these will do your baby a world of good. These oils are so important, that you should aim to add a teaspoon of cold-pressed seed oil to one meal each day for your baby – and for you. You can start with his or her first foods, with 1 teaspoon a day from 4 months old, increasing to 2 teaspoons from 6 months.

Always choose extra virgin olive oil as it is the juice extracted from the first pressing of olives (unlike virgin olive oil, which is made by mixing and refining much lower grade oil). Extra virgin olive oil is wonderful for us because of its high monounsaturated fat content in the form of oleic acid (between 60% and 80%), which studies have shown to reduce LDL cholesterol levels. Research has also linked oleic acid to a reduction in the growth of many types of cancer cells. Up to 20%

of extra virgin olive oil is also made up of essential omega-6 fatty acids. Added to this, the polyphenol antioxidants and vitamin E present in extra virgin olive oil make it a very healthy fat indeed.

Quinoa

Quinoa (pronounced keen-wah) is an ancient grain from South America. It is rich in protein, including all nine amino acids, and especially rich in lysine. Lysine is needed by the body for growth and repair so it is vital for growing children and all of us as we get older.

Quinoa is a good source of manganese, magnesium, iron, copper and phosphorus, which means it is important for people who suffer from migraines, diabetes and atherosclerosis. When cooked, quinoa has a fluffy, creamy texture and a slight nutty flavour, and works well as a replacement for rice and couscous.

Sardines

Sardines really are the best fish you can eat. Not only are so many fish these days being overfished, but many of them also contain dangerous levels of toxins because we pollute our oceans so badly. Farmed fish are not an option because they are raised in poor conditions, like intensively-farmed animals (with organic as the only exception). Sardines are so low down on the food chain that they don't carry toxins like other fish, especially large fish such as tuna.

Sardines are good for cardiovascular health, memory, joints, energy and skin. In addition, they are also a stunning source of omega-3 essential fats. If you start your baby on sardines young, he or she will love them. If you are not so keen on them, try the fishcakes on page 59. If you and your kids like sardines, try to slot them into your weekly routine. They are a great fast food and make an easy lunch served on toast with mayonnaise or on crispbreads.

Seaweeds

Dried seaweeds probably contain more minerals than any other kind of food. They are rich in essential minerals, vitamins, protein and important trace minerals – many of which are no longer in our exhausted soils. They contain all of the elements essential to health, including calcium, sodium, magnesium, potassium, iodine, iron and zinc. Seaweeds also contain important vitamins, including trace amounts of B12, which rarely occur in land vegetables.

If you've never used seaweed and don't understand it, now is a great time to add it to your ingredient list. I would suggest you start with two or three different kinds, such as kombu, nori and arame. If you buy these for your store cupboard, you will soon use them up as you try the recipes in this book.

If you want to cook your own beans, buy dried and cook them with kombu. Your kids will love nori straight from the packet or you can mix it with salads, pastas or rice dishes. Either buy sushi nori that is already toasted or buy plain and toast it quickly over a gas flame until it turns green. Arame can be used with courgette (see page 126) or can be crumbled, soaked and mixed into pasta or rice dishes without adding too strong a flavour.

Seeds

Seeds are nature's little powerhouses. They are loaded with protein and oil. Try adding them to yogurt, porridge or cereals for breakfast. Toss them into salads, pasta and rice dishes for lunch or dinner. And put little bowls of them out to encourage your children – and you – to snack on them during the day. You get their full benefit when you eat them raw, but toasting them lightly – or with tamari, if you wish – makes them pretty irresistible. If possible, store seeds in the refrigerator to keep them fresh so you receive the full benefit of their oils.

Sprouts

Packed with goodness, sprouts such as alfalfa, broccoli and mung contain an abundance of highly active antioxidants that prevent DNA destruction and protect us from the ongoing effects of ageing. They are also valued because they help to protect us from disease, increase bone formation and prevent bone breakdown, help control tumours and hot flushes, support the immune system – the list goes on and on.

Great tasting, sprouts can be used in many ways – use them to liven up a plain sandwich, add them to salads, use them in wraps, mix them with rice and include them in sushi. My daughter, Jessie, eats them

as a little salad on their own, tossed with olive oil and a little balsamic vinegar. If you have a good health food shop near you, you can find sprouts such as aduki, fenugreek, chickpea, lentil, mung, radish, sunflower and more. If not, they are easy to grow at home if you buy a sprouting kit.

Yogurt

The biggest reason to eat yogurt on a regular basis is for the good gut bacteria it contains. Forget those little yogurt drinks that are loaded with sugar. Eat plain full-fat yogurt as it has so much flavour and creaminess that you don't need sugar. Yogurt is an excellent source of protein, calcium, vitamin D, riboflavin, vitamin B6 and B12 – and much better to eat than milk because it has gone through a fermentation process that breaks down the milk sugar (lactose) and the milk protein (casein) for us. It also restores many of the enzymes, which are destroyed when milk is pasteurized, that help the body absorb calcium and other minerals. Eat it straight from the pot or add it to your cereal, mix it with muesli, toss it with fruit or add to desserts.

Getting started

Remember that how you prepare and cook foods can make a big difference to their nutritional qualities. I use methods you may not be familiar with, such as almost never peeling vegetables and always soaking whole grains (these methods are explained in more detail on pages 18–19 and 22–25).

What equipment do I need?
For prepping vegetables, buy a natural bristle vegetable scrubber because instead of peeling veggies, you'll be scrubbing them. Make sure you also have an excellent-quality knife for all of the cutting and chopping. For cooking, you'll need a few good stainless steel saucepans and frying pans, and some baking dishes (I avoid aluminium and most non-stick as there are questions over their safety). For steaming vegetables, a metal steamer is essential. For puréeing the baby's food, as well as making smoothies, breadcrumbs, bean dips and salsa, you'll need a small blender or food processor.

Keeping it clean
From 6 months old, I believe a little exposure to germs is a good thing. Babies who grow up in sterile environments have difficulty fighting infections and everyday colds. I don't bother with harsh, germ-killing cleaners because I don't want them around my family and I don't want to put them into the environment. I'm more afraid of the toxins in cleaners labelled with a skull and crossbones than I am of a few germs. Just make sure you always wash your hands before you cook, keep equipment clean, separate raw and cooked meats and cook eggs and meats thoroughly for young children.

Storing and freezing
Ceramic, glass or metal storage containers with lids are ideal for freezing the baby's food cubes. I stay away from plastic whenever possible as it contains harmful chemicals and pretty much never biodegrades. Any remaining food can be cooled, spooned into ice cube trays and frozen. When the cubes are solid, pop them out into another container, which you can date and label and store in the freezer for up to 3 months. You will soon build up a great selection of fruits, vegetables, grains, fish and meat from which you can pick and choose, either for a whole meal or to supplement something you have made fresh.

Food cubes quickly defrost and can be warmed in a small saucepan. Remember to defrost fish, poultry and meat in the fridge, and reheat rice thoroughly. You'll find the best way to feed your baby a good balance of different types of food is by cooking extra and freezing any leftovers. You can then add to any of the variations in the recipes with something from your freezer.

Steaming vegetables
It is best not to peel almost all vegetables, because of the nutrients and fibre in and just beneath the skin. And unless eating raw, it is best to steam vegetables

digested, the nutrients will be released and the difficult-to-digest complex sugars broken down.

Kombu helps soften beans, reduces the cooking time and makes them easier to digest. It can also be left in with the beans (except for babies) for added nutrition and flavour. Always add salt after beans have cooked, partly so you can separate the beans for the baby and partly because salt toughens the skins and inhibits the beans' cooking.

Other ideas

I've cooked for a long time, but no one ever told me this simple trick, which would have saved me making a number of mistakes and forgetting ingredients just because I was tired or distracted. When you have bought everything you need and are ready to cook, start by getting all of the ingredients out on the counter. Then prep your vegetables and such, as listed in the ingredients list. After that, follow the method. When you have completed the recipe, read back over the recipe and the ingredients list to ensure that you have followed every stage and used all the ingredients. It may save you from making frustrating mistakes.

Remember, if you can, to try and make food fun, too. If your child stops trying new things, make a game of it. Have them close their eyes and taste five or six different things. Remind them to try the foods with an open mind, not knowing what to expect or what the food might be. You can include something they really like in the selection.

I love cooking, but often I used to have no idea what to do for dinner. So, I now do two things. Firstly, I write down what I'm making for dinner every night for a week and buy the ingredients for those dishes. Secondly, I have a list of meals that we love to eat regularly for lunch and dinner, otherwise, I forget and tend to repeat foods too often. Don't be afraid to have the same foods on certain days, to make it easier for yourself. For example, we always have an eggy brunch on Sunday and pizza on Sunday night (it's my day off and this is what my husband likes to cook).

I also like to take a specific day each week to prepare for the week ahead. It's a day I commit to cooking and baking. I like to bake bread, a sweet baked good and a bean dip at least. And I do this on my grocery shopping day.

rather than boil them. And for babies, steaming is excellent. When you boil vegetables, a lot of the goodness goes into the water and is poured down the drain.

Pour water into a saucepan to a depth of 1cm/½in and bring to the boil. Put the vegetables in a steamer, put the steamer in the pan, cover and then steam for about 5 minutes until just tender, but with a little crunch. For babies, steam the vegetables for about 10 minutes (carrots for 20 minutes and squash for 30 minutes) until they are completely soft.

Soaking and cooking beans

Soaking beans in plenty of acidulated warm water (water with 1 tablespoon of lemon juice or vinegar) is an important step in their preparation. After they have soaked for at least 12 hours, rinse the beans well, boil hard in fresh water for 10 minutes, skimming any scum that rises to the surface, then cover and simmer with kombu (see page 17) until they are tender. This process ensures that the phytic acid will be neutralized, the beans will be easily

Ages & Stages

6–9 months

When your baby is ready to wean, start with the foods from the list below. Your baby may have some teeth now, but all foods should be puréed until completely smooth. Add water if necessary when puréeing, so that the texture of all foods is the consistency of yogurt.

If your baby is chewing, slowly add some finely grated raw fruits and vegetables (you can include skins, because they will be either puréed or finely grated). Give your baby breast milk or formula for breakfast and then only between meals, to encourage eating at mealtimes. You can now offer a little warm, filtered water with lunch and dinner.

Include 2 teaspoons of seed oil a day, alternating with olive oil.

At this age you can introduce fish, poultry and meats, although in small quantities. You can also bring in oats. Historically, oats were harvested, transported and processed by machines that handle grains containing gluten, so many people with gluten allergies kept away from them. When isolated, oats do not have gluten (they do contain a gluten-like protein that only very sensitive people react to). Buy gluten-free oats that are uncontaminated as they can be included in foods for 6–9 month old babies. Ideally, oats should always be soaked with yogurt or kefir (see page 22).

It's difficult to eat fish that is not overfished, as the list of species in danger changes regularly. I recommend anchovies (only fresh), mackerel (not King), salmon (wild or organic farmed) and sardines because they are oily fish and have lots of goodness. There are a few things to remember. Eat a variety – it wouldn't be good to feed your baby salmon all of the time, for example. And look for line-caught fish if you can find it. Avoid farmed fish, unless it is farmed organically – fish farming takes place under intensive conditions with the use of organophosphates, chlorine, antibiotics and other chemicals that are not good for your baby, you, the water or the land.

9–12 months

Your baby should be able to chew a little now, so food can be lumpier, you can add grated fruit or vegetables and you can serve little pieces (5mm/¼in) of fruit or vegetables, which will also encourage self-feeding. Make sure you sit with a baby who is eating small pieces of food in case he or she chokes. If your baby still isn't chewing much, don't worry and just continue to purée foods so that they will be properly digested.

Now come fruits with small seeds, some of the tougher, more fibrous vegetables and sprouts, which offer excellent

Foods to introduce at 6–9 months

- amaranth
- anchovy, fresh
- apple
- apricot
- artichoke heart
- avocado
- banana
- beef and red meats
- beetroot
- black bean
- black-eyed bean
- broad bean
- broccoli
- buckwheat
- butternut squash
- cannellini bean
- carrot
- cauliflower
- celeriac
- cherry
- chickpea
- coconut
- courgette
- flageolet bean
- flax seed oil
- green bean
- haricot bean
- hemp seed oil
- kefir, for soaking
- kombu, for cooking
- lemon juice, for soaking
- lentils (red, brown, large green, Puy)
- mackerel, not King
- mangetout
- mango
- millet
- mung bean
- nectarine
- oats (gluten-free)
- olive oil
- papaya
- parsnip
- pea
- peach
- pear
- pinto bean
- plum
- poultry
- prune
- pumpkin
- pumpkin seed oil
- quinoa
- rice (basmati, black, brown short/long grain, brown sushi, jasmine, red Camargue, Thai, wild)
- safflower oil
- salmon
- sardine
- sesame oil
- sunflower oil
- swede
- sweet potato
- turnip
- venison and game
- yogurt, for soaking

Foods to introduce at 9–12 months

- asparagus
- blackberry
- blueberry
- butter
- Chinese leaf
- cornflour/cornmeal
- cranberry, unsweetened
- cucumber
- currant
- date
- fennel
- fig
- fresh herbs, such as basil, mint and parsley
- garlic
- grape
- haddock
- Jerusalem artichoke
- kefir
- kiwi
- leek
- lychee
- oats
- onion
- pak choi
- polenta
- pollock
- raisin
- raspberry
- rhubarb
- spring onion
- sprouts (all types, including alfalfa, broccoli, chickpea, lentil, mung and radish)
- trout
- yogurt

nutrition. You can now also introduce natural yogurt and small amounts of butter. Carry on with 2 teaspoons of seed and/or olive oil per day.

From 12 months on

At 12 months your child can eat all family meals. You can offer strawberries and citrus in small quantities. It is also okay now to start with the deadly nightshade family (aubergine, mushroom, potato, tomato and sweet pepper) and some gluten-containing grains. Egg and soya can be introduced, keeping soya products to a minimum and favouring tempeh over soya.

You can go ahead with wheat (although keeping it to a minimum is a good idea), nuts (except peanuts until 5 years) and seeds are allowed – just make sure they are being chewed well – and organic cheese can be eaten, focusing on sheep's and goat's cheese in preference to cow's.

As well as continuing with 2 teaspoons of seed or olive oil per day, you can make an essential fatty acid (EFA) seed mix. Put 1 measure each of sesame seeds and your choice of either sunflower or pumpkin seeds in a jar. Add 2 measures of flax seeds, seal tightly and keep in the fridge away from light, heat and air. Grind 1 teaspoon of the mixture in a spice mill or coffee grinder at mealtimes and mix it with your child's food. You can alternate this with the oils.

From 12 months, your child can eat everything, including:

- almond
- aubergine
- barley
- Brazil nut
- Brussels sprout
- cabbage
- caper
- cashew nut
- celery
- chard
- cheese, especially organic goat's and sheep's milk
- chestnut
- clementine
- edamame bean
- eggs
- flax seeds, ground
- gherkin
- grapefruit
- hazelnut
- hemp seeds, ground
- kale
- Kamut
- kumquat
- lemon
- lettuce
- lime
- macadamia nut
- mandarin
- mushroom
- olives, pitted
- orange
- passion fruit
- pecan
- pepper (red, yellow, orange, green)
- pine nut
- pistachio nut
- pomegranate
- pomelo
- potato
- pumpkin seeds, ground
- rocket
- rye
- samphire
- satsuma
- seaweed (arame, hijiki, kombu, nori)
- sesame seeds, ground
- soya, including tempeh and tofu
- spelt
- spinach
- strawberry
- sunflower seeds, ground
- sweetcorn
- tangelo
- tangerine
- tomato
- walnut
- watercress
- wheat

Basic recipes

These pages contain all of the basic recipes for cooking grains and beans. Because you may be using these recipes often, you might want to photocopy these pages – or the one you use the most – and stick them on your fridge or cupboard.

 The methods say to soak grains and rice for at least 7 hours. If you remember the night before, then put grains to soak then, because the extra soaking time will only be an improvement. If, however, you forget, then you still have time to put something to soak in the morning for a meal you are cooking that evening. If you don't remember until the afternoon, make the meal anyway, but do try to get into the excellent habit of soaking grains.

 The recipe cooking times that follow are for adults. You must add on 20 minutes if you are cooking any grains for your baby and add an extra 125ml/4fl oz/½ cup warm water to the pan. Rice for an adult should be cooked until it retains a slight bite, but for babies, should be completely soft.

 If these recipes require seasoning, then add 1 teaspoon of fine sea salt for each 1 cup of uncooked grain or bean.

GRAINS

COOKED MILLET

....

PREPARATION: 5 minutes, plus at least 7 hours soaking
COOKING TIME: 20 minutes

100g/3½oz/½ cup millet
½ tsp natural yogurt or kefir

1 Put the millet, yogurt and 500ml/17fl oz/2 cups warm water in a saucepan and leave to soak, covered, for 7 hours or overnight at room temperature.

2 Bring to the boil over a high heat, then turn the heat down to low and simmer, covered, for 20 minutes until soft.

COOKED BUCKWHEAT

....

PREPARATION: 5 minutes, plus at least 7 hours soaking
COOKING TIME: 20 minutes

60g/2¼oz/⅓ cup buckwheat
1 tbsp natural yogurt or kefir

1 Put the buckwheat, yogurt and 310ml/10¾fl oz/ 1¼ cups warm water in a saucepan and leave to soak, covered, for 7 hours or overnight at room temperature.

2 Bring to the boil over a high heat, then turn the heat down to low and simmer, covered, for 20 minutes until completely soft.

COOKED OAT PORRIDGE

....

PREPARATION: 5 minutes, plus at least 7 hours soaking
COOKING TIME: 10 minutes

100g/3½oz/1 cup porridge oats
1 tbsp natural yogurt or kefir

1 Put the oats, yogurt and 750ml/26fl oz/3 cups warm water in a saucepan and leave to soak, covered, for 7 hours or overnight at room temperature.

2 Bring to a simmer over a medium heat, then turn the heat down to low and simmer, stirring occasionally, for 10 minutes until soft and creamy.

COOKED QUINOA OR RED QUINOA

....

PREPARATION: 5 minutes, plus at least 7 hours soaking
COOKING TIME: 20 minutes

200g/7oz/1 cup quinoa or red quinoa
1 tbsp natural yogurt or kefir

1 Put the quinoa, yogurt and 750ml/26fl oz/3 cups warm water in a saucepan and leave to soak, covered, for 7 hours or overnight at room temperature.

2 Bring to the boil over a high heat, then turn the heat down to low and simmer, covered, for 20 minutes until tender.

COOKED BROWN BASMATI RICE

PREPARATION: 5 minutes, plus at least 7 hours soaking
COOKING TIME: 35 minutes

200g/7oz/1 cup brown basmati rice
1 tbsp natural yogurt or kefir

1 Put the rice, yogurt and 455ml/16fl oz/scant 2 cups warm water in a saucepan and leave to soak, covered, for 7 hours or overnight at room temperature.

2 Bring to the boil over a high heat, then turn the heat down to low and simmer, covered, for 35 minutes until the rice is just cooked but still retains a slight bite.

COOKED BROWN RICE, BROWN SUSHI RICE OR BROWN SHORT GRAIN RICE, RED CAMARGUE RICE

PREPARATION: 5 minutes, plus at least 7 hours soaking
COOKING TIME: 40 minutes

200g/7oz/1 cup brown rice, brown sushi rice or brown short grain rice, red Camargue rice
1 tbsp natural yogurt or kefir

1 Put the rice, yogurt and 455ml/16fl oz/scant 2 cups warm water in a saucepan and leave to soak, covered, for 7 hours or overnight at room temperature.

2 Bring to the boil over a high heat, then turn the heat down to low and simmer, covered, for 40 minutes until the rice is just cooked but still retains a slight bite.

COOKED WILD RICE

PREPARATION: 5 minutes, plus at least 7 hours soaking
COOKING TIME: 40 minutes

75g/2½oz/½ cup wild rice
½ tbsp natural yogurt or kefir

1 Put the wild rice, yogurt and 250ml/9fl oz/1 cup warm water in a saucepan and leave to soak, covered, for 7 hours or overnight at room temperature.

2 Bring to the boil over a high heat, then turn the heat down to low and simmer, covered, for 40 minutes until the rice is just cooked but still retains a slight bite.

DRIED BEANS & LENTILS

COOKED DRIED BLACK BEANS

PREPARATION: 5 minutes, plus at least 12 hours soaking
COOKING TIME: 1 hour 40 minutes

100g/3½oz/½ cup black (turtle) beans
½ tbsp lemon juice, grape vinegar or white wine vinegar
½ strip of kombu, about 8 x 5cm/3¼ x 2in (optional)

1 Put the black beans in a saucepan. Add the lemon juice, cover generously with warm water and leave to soak, covered, for 12 hours or overnight at room temperature.

2 Drain and rinse the beans, then return them to the pan. Add 375ml/13fl oz/1½ cups water and bring to the boil over a high heat. Boil for 10 minutes, skimming any scum that rises to the surface, then turn the heat down to low and add the kombu, if using. Simmer, covered, for 1½ hours until soft. Check occasionally to ensure that the beans remain covered with water and add extra boiling water if necessary. Remove the kombu from the pan and reserve for chopping or mashing. Drain the beans.

COOKED DRIED CANNELLINI BEANS

PREPARATION: 5 minutes, plus at least 12 hours soaking
COOKING TIME: 1 hour 10 minutes

100g/3½oz/½ cup dried cannellini beans
½ tbsp lemon juice, grape vinegar or white wine vinegar
½ strip of kombu, about 8 x 5cm/3¼ x 2in (optional)

1 Put the cannellini beans in a saucepan. Add the lemon juice, cover generously with warm water and leave to soak, covered, for 12 hours or overnight at room temperature.

2 Drain and rinse the beans, then return them to the pan. Add 1.2l/40fl oz/4¾ cups water and bring to the boil over a high heat. Boil for 10 minutes, skimming any scum that rises to the surface, then turn the heat down to low and add the kombu, if using. Simmer, covered, for 1 hour until soft. Check occasionally to ensure that the beans remain covered with water and add extra boiling water if necessary. Remove the kombu from the pan and reserve for chopping or mashing. Drain the beans.

COOKED DRIED CHICKPEAS

PREPARATION: 5 minutes, plus at least 12 hours soaking
COOKING TIME: 2 hours 10 minutes

100g/3½oz/½ cup dried chickpeas
½ tbsp lemon juice, grape vinegar or white wine vinegar
½ strip of kombu, about 8 x 5cm/3¼ x 2in (optional)

1 Put the chickpeas in a saucepan. Add the lemon juice, cover generously with warm water and leave to soak, covered, for 12 hours or overnight at room temperature.

2 Drain and rinse the chickpeas, then return them to the pan. Add 1.4l/48fl oz/5½ cups water and bring to the boil over a high heat. Boil for 10 minutes, skimming any scum that rises to the surface, then turn the heat down to low and add the kombu, if using. Simmer, covered, for 2 hours until soft. Check occasionally to ensure that the chickpeas remain covered with water and add extra boiling water if necessary. Remove the kombu from the pan and reserve for chopping or mashing. Drain the chickpeas.

COOKED DRIED HARICOT BEANS

PREPARATION: 5 minutes, plus at least 12 hours soaking
COOKING TIME: 1 hour 40 minutes

200g/7oz/1 cup haricot beans
1 tbsp lemon juice, grape vinegar or white wine vinegar
1 strip of kombu, 16 x 10cm/6¼ x 4in (optional)

1 Put the haricot beans in a saucepan. Add the lemon juice, cover generously with warm water and leave to soak, covered, for 12 hours or overnight at room temperature.

2 Drain and rinse the beans, then return them to the pan. Add 1.2l/40fl oz/4¾ cups water and bring to the boil over a high heat. Boil for 10 minutes, skimming

any scum that rises to the surface, then turn the heat down to low and add the kombu, if using. Simmer, covered, for 1½ hours until soft. Check occasionally to ensure that the beans remain covered with water and add extra boiling water if necessary. Remove the kombu from the pan and reserve for chopping or mashing. Drain the beans.

COOKED DRIED KIDNEY BEANS

PREPARATION: 5 minutes, plus at least 12 hours soaking
COOKING TIME: 1 hour 40 minutes

180g/6¼oz/1 cup kidney beans
1 tbsp lemon juice, grape vinegar or white wine vinegar
1 strip of kombu, 16 x 10cm/6¼ x 4in (optional)

1 Put the kidney beans in a saucepan. Add the lemon juice, cover generously with warm water and leave to soak, covered, for 12 hours or overnight at room temperature.

2 Drain and rinse the beans, then return them to the pan. Add 1l/35fl oz/4 cups water and bring to the boil over a high heat. Boil for 10 minutes, skimming any scum that rises to the surface, then turn the heat down to low and add the kombu, if using. Simmer, covered, for 1½ hours until soft. Check occasionally to ensure that the beans remain covered with water and add extra boiling water if necessary. Remove the kombu from the pan and reserve for chopping or mashing. Drain the beans.

COOKED MUNG BEANS

PREPARATION: 5 minutes, plus at least 12 hours soaking
COOKING TIME: 55 minutes

100g/3½oz/½ cup mung beans
½ tbsp lemon juice, grape vinegar or white wine vinegar
½ strip of kombu, about 8 x 5cm/3¼ x 2in (optional)

1 Put the mung beans in a saucepan. Add the lemon juice, cover generously with warm water and leave to soak, covered, for 12 hours or overnight at room temperature.

2 Drain and rinse the beans, then return them to the pan. Add 750ml/26fl oz/3 cups water and bring to the boil over a high heat. Boil for 10 minutes, skimming any scum that rises to the surface, then turn the heat down to low and add the kombu, if using. Simmer, covered, for 45 minutes until soft. Check occasionally to ensure that the beans remain covered with water and add extra boiling water if necessary. Remove kombu from the pan and reserve for chopping or mashing. Drain the beans.

COOKED DRIED PINTO BEANS

PREPARATION: 5 minutes, plus at least 12 hours soaking
COOKING TIME: 1 hour 40 minutes

200g/7oz/1 cup pinto beans
1½ tbsp lemon juice, grape vinegar or white wine vinegar
1 strip of kombu, 16x10cm/6¼ x 4in (optional)

1 Put the pinto beans in a saucepan. Add the lemon juice, cover generously with warm water and leave to soak, covered, for 12 hours or overnight at room temperature.

2 Drain and rinse the beans, then return them to the pan. Add 1.5l/52fl oz/6 cups water and bring to the boil over a high heat. Boil for 10 minutes, skimming any scum that rises to the surface, then turn the heat down to low and add the kombu, if using. Simmer, covered, for 1½ hours until soft. Check occasionally to ensure that the beans remain covered with water and add extra boiling water if necessary. Remove the kombu from the pan and reserve for chopping or mashing. Drain the beans.

COOKED LARGE GREEN LENTILS

PREPARATION: 5 minutes, plus at least 12 hours soaking
COOKING TIME: 30 minutes

200g/7oz/1 cup large green lentils
1 tbsp lemon juice, grape vinegar or white wine vinegar
1 strip of kombu, 16 x 10cm/6¼ x 4in (optional)

1 Put the lentils in a saucepan. Add the lemon juice, cover generously with warm water and leave to soak, covered, for 12 hours or overnight at room temperature.

2 Drain and rinse the lentils, then return them to the pan. Add 875ml/30fl oz/3½ cups water and bring to the boil over a high heat, then turn the heat down to low and add the kombu to the pan, if using. Simmer, covered, for 30 minutes until soft and starting to break up. Remove the kombu from the pan and reserve for chopping or mashing. Drain the lentils.

SOAKED BROWN OR PUY LENTILS

PREPARATION: 5 minutes, plus at least 7 hours soaking

200g/7oz/1 cup brown lentils or Puy lentils
1 tbsp lemon juice, grape vinegar or white wine vinegar

1 Put the lentils in a saucepan. Add the lemon juice, cover generously with warm water and leave to soak, covered, for 7 hours or overnight at room temperature. Drain and rinse the lentils.

chapter one
start the day well

I love breakfast because it's a brilliant opportunity to get something wonderful into your baby or your kids, as everyone usually wakes up hungry. There are recipes here for rushed mornings when you're short on time, like the Pear & Pecan Smoothie. This recipe then gives you a Pear & Brown Rice Purée for a 6–9 month old and Pear, Rice & Yogurt Mix for a 9–12 month old.

For mornings when you have planned ahead, there are lovely soaked porridges made from fabulous grains like amaranth or millet. And for the leisurely weekends when you get up with nowhere you have to be, you can mix up some American-style Three-Grain Pancakes with Papaya. Forget those sugary breakfast cereals and discover wonderful dishes to start the day well. You'll also find breakfast breads in chapter four.

Whizzing up a smoothie in the blender is an easy way to make breakfast quickly. The pecans add protein, essential oil and a creamy richness. And it's easier to get some children to eat fruit if it's puréed into a yummy drink.

Pear & Pecan Smoothie

SERVES: 2 adults, 1 child and 1 baby
PREPARATION TIME: 5 minutes
STORAGE: Refrigerate for up to 3 days.

....

2 large pears, cored and roughly chopped
40g/1½oz/heaped ⅓ cup pecans
500ml/17fl oz/2 cups oat milk, or rice milk
150g/5½oz/scant ⅔ cup natural yogurt
6 tbsp instant baby wholegrain rice flakes

1 (6-9) (9-12) Put all the ingredients in a blender and blend for 30 seconds until smooth. Pour into glasses and serve.

(6-9) **PEAR & BROWN RICE PURÉE**
Put 9 pear pieces, 3 tablespoons of the rice flakes powder and 8 tablespoons water in a blender. Blend for 30 seconds, adding extra water 1 teaspoon at a time, until smooth. Serve warm or at room temperature.

(9-12) **PEAR, RICE & YOGURT MIX**
Put 9 pear pieces, 2 tablespoons of the rice flakes powder, 2 tablespoons of the yogurt and 4 tablespoons water in a blender. Pulse for 15 seconds, adding extra water 1 teaspoon at a time, until the mixture forms a lumpy purée. Serve warm or at room temperature.

This is great for kids – or when you have guests to stay. Combined with fresh or dried fruit, nuts and seeds, the yogurt mixture is nourishing and sustaining. Put a selection of ingredients out for everyone to sprinkle in their bowl and create their own flavour combinations.

Fruit & Nut Medley with Yogurt

SERVES: 2 adults, 1 child and 1 baby
PREPARATION TIME: 10 minutes
STORAGE: Refrigerate for up to 3 days.

....

150g/5½oz/scant 1¼ cups raisins
2 nectarines, pitted and chopped
40g/1½oz/heaped ⅓ cup ground
    almonds
4 tbsp desiccated coconut
4 tsp sunflower seeds
4 tsp linseeds
500g/1lb 2oz/2 cups natural yogurt

1 Put the raisins and 150ml/5fl oz/scant ⅔ cup boiling water in a heatproof bowl and leave to soften for 5 minutes.

2 (6-9) (9-12) Put the nectarines, ground almonds, coconut and seeds in a large bowl. Drain the raisins and discard the soaking water, then add them to the bowl and mix in. Add the yogurt, mix well and serve.

 (6-9) **NECTARINE PURÉE**
Put ¼ of the nectarines and 2 tablespoons water in a blender. Blend for 30 seconds, adding extra water 1 teaspoon at a time, until smooth. Serve warm or at room temperature.

(9-12) **NECTARINE, RAISIN & YOGURT MIX**
Put ¼ of the nectarines, 1 tablespoon of the soaked raisins, 2 tablespoons of the yogurt and 1 tablespoon water in a blender. Pulse for 15 seconds, adding extra water 1 teaspoon at a time, until the mixture forms a lumpy purée. Serve warm or at room temperature.

I love soaking muesli with yogurt because it becomes very creamy. It also makes muesli more digestible and means that the minerals in the muesli, such as iron, magnesium, calcium and zinc are absorbed more easily by your body. You can double this recipe and store the dried mix in a jar.

Swiss Muesli

SERVES: 2 adults, 1 child and 1 baby
PREPARATION TIME: 20 minutes, plus overnight soaking
STORAGE: Refrigerate soaked muesli for up to 3 days.

. . . .

150g/5½oz/1½ cups porridge oats
50g/1¾oz/½ cup millet (or any other grain) flakes
30g/1oz/¼ cup raisins
30g/1oz/¼ cup dried cranberries
2 tbsp flaked almonds
2 tbsp roughly chopped hazelnuts
2 tbsp sunflower seeds
2 tbsp linseeds
3 tbsp natural yogurt or kefir
1 apple

1 (6-9) (9-12) Mix the oats, millet flakes, raisins, cranberries, almonds, hazelnuts and seeds in a large bowl. Add the yogurt and 625ml/21½fl oz/2½ cups warm water and mix well. Leave to soak, covered, overnight at room temperature.

2 Core and grate the apple, then mix into the muesli and serve.

(6-9) OAT & APPLE PURÉE
Put 4 tablespoons of the oats, ½ teaspoon of the yogurt and 185ml/6fl oz/¾ cup warm water in a saucepan and leave to soak, covered, overnight at room temperature. Bring to a simmer over a medium heat, then turn the heat down to low and cook, stirring occasionally, for 10 minutes until completely soft. Transfer to a blender and add ½ of the grated apple and 2 tablespoons water. Blend for 30 seconds, adding extra water 1 teaspoon at a time, until smooth. Serve warm.

(9-12) FRUIT & OAT MIX
Put 4 tablespoons of the oats, 1 teaspoon of the raisins, 1 teaspoon of the cranberries, 1 teaspoon of the yogurt and 185ml/6fl oz/¾ cup warm water in a saucepan and leave to soak, covered, overnight at room temperature. Bring to a simmer over a medium heat, then turn the heat down to low and cook, stirring occasionally, for 10 minutes until completely soft. Transfer to a blender and add 2 tablespoons water. Pulse for 15 seconds, adding extra water 1 teaspoon at a time, until the mixture forms a lumpy purée. Mix 1 tablespoon of the grated apple into the oat mixture and serve warm.

Dried mango adds a lovely sweetness and a host of wonderful nutrients to this breakfast. It's worth slotting amaranth into your repertoire of grains and breakfasts: it's a good source of protein and an excellent source of calcium – which you and your kids need.

Amaranth with Mango

SERVES: 2 adults, 1 child and 1 baby
PREPARATION TIME: 10 minutes, plus at least 7 hours soaking (optional)
COOKING TIME: 40 minutes
STORAGE: Refrigerate for up to 3 days.

....

100g/3½oz/½ cup amaranth
2½ tbsp natural yogurt or kefir, for soaking (optional)
30g/1oz/scant ¼ cup dried mango, chopped

1 (9-18) If soaking the amaranth, put the amaranth, yogurt and 600ml/21fl oz/scant 2½ cups warm water in a large saucepan. Add the mango and mix well. Leave to soak, covered, for 7 hours or overnight at room temperature.

2 Bring to the boil over a high heat. Turn the heat down to low and cook, covered, for 40 minutes, stirring occasionally, until the amaranth is completely soft and cooked through.

(If cooking unsoaked amaranth, put the amaranth and 600ml/21fl oz/scant 2½ cups water in a large saucepan. Mix in the mango and bring to the boil over a high heat. Turn the heat down to low and cook, covered, for 40 minutes, stirring occasionally, until the amaranth is completely soft and cooked through.)

3 (6-9) Remove from the heat and serve warm.

(6-9)

AMARANTH & MANGO PURÉE
Put 4 tablespoons of the cooked amaranth and mango mixture and 2 tablespoons water in a blender. Blend for 30 seconds, adding extra water 1 teaspoon at a time, until smooth. Serve warm.

(9-12)

AMARANTH, MANGO & YOGURT MIX
Put 4 tablespoons of the cooked amaranth and mango mixture, 2 tablespoons of the yogurt and 1 tablespoon water in a blender. Pulse for 15 seconds, adding extra water 1 teaspoon at a time, until the mixture forms a lumpy purée. Serve warm.

When I first made this, my husband Brian pulled a face and reached for the muesli instead. But when he tried it, he loved the combination of creamy millet and crunchy nuts with the sweetness of dates and rice malt syrup.

Millet Simmer with Dates & Hazelnuts

SERVES: 2 adults, 1 child and 1 baby
PREPARATION TIME: 10 minutes, plus at least 7 hours soaking and 20 minutes cooking the millet
STORAGE: Refrigerate for up to 3 days.

....

20g/¾oz/scant ¼ cup hazelnuts
1 recipe quantity cooked millet (see page 22)
125g/4½oz/½ cup natural yogurt
4 dates, pitted and finely chopped
3 tbsp rice malt syrup or 2½ tbsp cane sugar

1 Put the hazelnuts in a plastic bag and break into small pieces with a rolling pin. (6-9) (9-12) Transfer to a bowl, add the cooked millet, yogurt, dates and rice malt syrup and mix until warmed through, then serve.

(6-9) **MILLET PORRIDGE PURÉE**
Put 4 tablespoons of the cooked millet and 135ml/4½fl oz/generous ½ cup boiling water in a saucepan and simmer, covered, over a low heat for 20 minutes until completely soft. Transfer to a blender and add 2 tablespoons water. Blend for 30 seconds, adding extra water 1 teaspoon at a time, until smooth. Serve warm.

(9-12) **MILLET & DATE PORRIDGE**
Put 4 tablespoons of the cooked millet, ½ tablespoon of the dates and 135ml/4½fl oz/generous ½ cup boiling water in a saucepan and simmer, covered, over a low heat for 20 minutes until completely soft. Transfer to a blender and add 2 tablespoons water. Pulse for 15 seconds, adding extra water 1 teaspoon at a time, until the mixture forms a lumpy purée. Serve warm.

On weekends when you have a little more time, this is a lovely breakfast treat. With a crispy crust on the outside and delicate dough on the inside, it's a favourite with everyone. My kids love it because they feel like they're having pie for breakfast.

Baked Apple Puff

SERVES: 2 adults, 1 child and 1 baby
PREPARATION TIME: 15 minutes
COOKING TIME: 25 minutes
STORAGE: Store in an airtight container for up to 2 days.

....

3 large eggs
150ml/5fl oz/scant ⅔ cup oat milk, rice milk or water
60g/2¼oz/½ cup wholemeal spelt flour or wholemeal plain flour
2½ tbsp rice malt syrup or 2 tbsp cane sugar
½ tsp vanilla extract
1 tsp ground cinnamon
¼ tsp fine sea salt
15g/½oz unsalted butter
2 apples, cored and thinly sliced

1 Preheat the oven to 200°C/400°F/gas 6. In a large mixing bowl, lightly beat the eggs together with a whisk. (9-12) Add the oat milk, flour, rice malt syrup, vanilla extract, cinnamon and salt and whisk until smooth.

2 Melt the butter in a 25cm/10in flameproof pie dish in the oven. Remove from the oven and tilt the pie dish to evenly coat the base in melted butter. (6-9) Pour the batter into the pie dish and arrange the apples on top. Bake for 25 minutes until lightly browned. Serve warm.

(6-9) BAKED APPLE PURÉE
Chop 10 apple slices into small pieces. Put the apple and 1 tablespoon water in a small ramekin and bake as above for 15 minutes until the apple is completely soft. Transfer to a blender and blend for 30 seconds, adding water 1 teaspoon at a time, until smooth. Serve warm.

(9-12) BAKED CINNAMON APPLE
Chop 10 apple slices into small pieces. Put the apple, 1 tablespoon of the oat milk, 1 teaspoon of the melted butter and a pinch of the cinnamon in a small ramekin and bake as above for 15 minutes until the apple is completely soft. Transfer to a blender and pulse for 15 seconds, adding water 1 teaspoon at a time, until the mixture forms a lumpy purée. Serve warm.

Saturday pancakes are a family tradition. I like to mix the oat milk, grains and yogurt the night before and leave them at room temperature to ferment a little. In the morning, just mix in the other ingredients.

Three-Grain Pancakes with Papaya

MAKES: 12 pancakes
PREPARATION TIME: 20 minutes
COOKING TIME: 18 minutes
STORAGE: Refrigerate the uncooked batter for up to 1 day. Refrigerate the pancakes for up to 3 days.

....

1 papaya, peeled, deseeded and
    roughly chopped
1 egg
200ml/7fl oz/scant 1 cup oat milk,
    rice milk or water
3 tbsp sunflower oil, plus extra
    for frying if needed
50g/1¾oz/⅓ cup buckwheat flour
90g/3¼oz/¾ cup wholemeal spelt
    flour or wholemeal plain flour
55g/2oz/⅓ cup fast-cook polenta
1½ tsp baking powder
½ tsp fine sea salt
unsalted butter and maple syrup,
    to serve (optional), or 1 lemon,
    cut into wedges and cane sugar,
    to serve (optional)

1 Put the papaya in a blender and blend, adding water 1 tablespoon at a time, until smooth, then transfer to a bowl and set aside.

2 In a large bowl, lightly beat the egg with a whisk. Add the oat milk and 1 tablespoon of the oil and whisk. In another bowl, mix together the flours, polenta, baking powder and salt. Add the flour mixture to the egg mixture and whisk until smooth.

3 Preheat the oven to 100°C/200°F/gas ½. Heat the remaining oil in a large, heavy-based frying pan, or heat a griddle pan, over a medium-low heat. Working in batches, pour 2 tablespoons of the batter into the pan to make a pancake and repeat, spacing the pancakes slightly apart. Cook for 2–3 minutes on each side or until the bubbles that appear on the surface pop and the undersides of the pancakes are lightly browned. Keep warm in the oven while you repeat with the remaining batter, adding more oil to the pan as needed.

4 Serve hot with the papaya purée. Alternatively, serve with a little butter spread on top and drizzled with maple syrup, or sprinkle with freshly squeezed lemon juice and sugar.

(6-9) PAPAYA PURÉE
Put 5 tablespoons of the papaya purée in a bowl and serve warm or at room temperature.

(9-12) BUCKWHEAT PANCAKES WITH PAPAYA PURÉE
Mix together 2 tablespoons of the buckwheat flour and 3 tablespoons water in a small bowl to form a smooth paste. Heat 1 tablespoon of the oil in a heavy-based frying pan over a medium-low heat. Pour the batter into the pan to make a pancake and cook for 1–2 minutes on each side until the bubbles that appear on the surface pop and the underside of the pancake is lightly browned. Transfer to a blender and add 2 tablespoons water. Pulse for 15 seconds, adding extra water 1 teaspoon at a time, until the mixture forms a lumpy purée. Serve warm with 2 tablespoons of the papaya purée.

When you've got bananas that are getting old, either make these simple hotcakes or Banana Walnut Bread (see page 143). Great just with butter, these are naturally sweet and satisfying. Loved by young and old, bananas are an excellent source of potassium, an essential mineral.

Banana Hotcakes

MAKES: 12
PREPARATION TIME: 15 minutes
COOKING TIME: 18 minutes
STORAGE: Use the same day.

....

2 large eggs
4 bananas
2 tbsp natural yogurt
80g/2¾oz/⅔ cup wholemeal spelt flour or wholemeal plain flour
50g/1¾oz/½ cup porridge oats
1 tsp baking powder
30g/1oz unsalted butter, plus extra for frying if needed and to serve

1 In a small bowl, lightly beat the eggs together with a whisk. (9-12) In a large mixing bowl, mash the bananas, using a fork, until smooth. (6-9) Add the eggs, yogurt, flour, oats and baking powder and mix until well combined.

2 Heat a large, heavy-based frying pan or griddle pan over a medium-low heat until hot. Add the butter and heat until melted, tilting the pan to evenly coat the base. Working in batches, pour 2 tablespoons of the batter into the pan and repeat, spacing the hotcakes slightly apart. Cook for 2–3 minutes on each side until lightly browned. Repeat with the remaining batter, adding more butter to the pan as needed. Serve warm with a little butter spread on top.

(6-9) **OAT & BANANA PURÉE**
Put 4 tablespoons of the oats, 1 teaspoon of the yogurt and 185ml/6fl oz/ ¾ cup warm water in a saucepan and leave to soak, covered, for 7 hours or overnight at room temperature. Bring to the boil over a high heat, then turn the heat down to low and, simmer, covered, for 10 minutes, stirring occasionally, until completely soft. Put the porridge, 2 tablespoons of the mashed banana and 2 tablespoons water in a blender. Blend for 30 seconds, adding extra water 1 teaspoon at a time, until smooth. Serve warm.

(9-12) **FRIED BANANA COINS**
Slice ½ of 1 banana into thick coins. Heat 1 teaspoon of the butter in a frying pan over a medium heat until melted. Add the bananas and fry for 3 minutes on each side until the bananas are completely soft and lightly browned. Serve warm.

This nutrient-packed breakfast combines protein with complex carbohydrates and fresh fruit. Very quick to make, they will nourish and sustain you through the morning. If I eat these when I'm up early with the kids, I don't feel my first tummy rumble until midday.

Fried Peach Fritters

MAKES: 12
PREPARATION TIME: 10 minutes, plus at least 7 hours soaking and 10 minutes cooking the porridge
COOKING TIME: 25 minutes
STORAGE: Refrigerate for up to 3 days.

....

2 large eggs
1 recipe quantity cooked oat porridge (see page 22)
3 tbsp wholemeal spelt flour or wholemeal plain flour
2 peaches, pitted and finely chopped
½ tsp fine sea salt
30g/1oz unsalted butter, plus extra for frying if needed

1 In a large mixing bowl, lightly beat the eggs together with a whisk. **6-9** **9-12** Add the cooked oat porridge, flour, peaches and salt and mix well.

2 Heat the butter in a large, heavy-based frying pan over a medium-high heat until melted, tilting the pan to evenly coat the base. Working in batches, pour 2 tablespoons of the batter into the pan to make a fritter and repeat, spacing the fritters slightly apart. Cook for 4–5 minutes on each side until the fritters are lightly browned and crisp around the edges. If they break as you try to lift them, give them another minute or so to cook. Repeat with the remaining batter, adding more butter to the pan as needed. Serve hot.

6-9 **PEACH PORRIDGE PURÉE**
Put ¼ of the peaches, 4 tablespoons of the cooked oat porridge and 2 tablespoons water in a blender. Blend for 30 seconds, adding extra water 1 teaspoon at a time, until smooth. Serve warm.

 FRIED PEACH PORRIDGE
Put ¼ of the peaches and 4 tablespoons of the cooked oat porridge in a blender. Pulse for 15 seconds until the mixture forms a lumpy purée. Heat 1 teaspoon of the butter in a frying pan over a medium heat until melted. Add the peach and porridge mixture and cook, stirring occasionally, for 4–5 minutes until lightly browned. Serve warm.

Salmon and eggs are a winning combination. If you sleep in late after a difficult night or it's a lazy weekend for everyone, this is a great, protein-rich dish for you and your little one first thing. Toddlers and older children love eating out of their own little ramekin.

Mini Salmon Egg Bakes

MAKES: 6
PREPARATION TIME: 30 minutes
COOKING TIME: 18 minutes
STORAGE: Refrigerate for up to 1 day.

....

extra virgin olive oil, for greasing
1 onion, finely chopped
150g/5½oz boneless, skinless
    salmon fillets, roughly chopped
6 large eggs
1 tbsp Dijon mustard
a large pinch of cayenne pepper
¾ tsp fine sea salt
freshly ground black pepper
buttered toast, to serve

1 Preheat the oven to 200°C/400°F/gas 6 and grease six ramekins with oil.

2 (6-9) (9-12) Divide the onion and salmon evenly into the ramekins and set aside. In a bowl, beat the eggs together with a whisk. Add the mustard, cayenne pepper and salt, season with black pepper and mix well. Pour the egg mixture evenly into the ramekins.

3 Put the ramekins in a deep baking dish and fill the dish with enough boiling water to come halfway up the sides of the ramekins. Bake for 15–18 minutes until firm to the touch and very lightly browned. Serve warm with buttered toast.

(6-9)

SALMON PURÉE
Heat a frying pan over a medium-low heat until hot. Add 50g/1¾oz of the salmon and 1 tablespoon water and cook, covered, for 10 minutes until the salmon is opaque and completely cooked through. Transfer to a blender and add 2 tablespoons water. Blend for 30 seconds, adding extra water 1 teaspoon at a time, until smooth. Serve warm.

(9-12)

SALMON & ONION MIX
Heat a frying pan over a medium-low heat until hot. Add 50g/1¾oz of the salmon, 1 tablespoon of the onion and 1 tablespoon water. Cook, stirring occasionally, for 10 minutes until the salmon is opaque and completely cooked through and the onion is soft. Transfer to a blender and add 2 tablespoons water. Pulse for 15 seconds, adding extra water 1 teaspoon at a time, until the mixture forms a lumpy purée. Serve warm.

chapter two
time for lunch

Lunchtime is a great opportunity to take a little bit of time out of your hectic day and sit with your family. Here you'll find a wide selection of recipes to fill them with delicious, nourishing food – all easy to make, and all with variations for your baby.

Try the ingenious recipe for Chicken, Ham & Cheesy Pasta, for example. No need to make a separate cheese sauce, or to cook the vegetables first. What's more, you can whizz up a Chicken, Broccoli & Cauliflower Pasta Purée for a 6–9 month old, or a Chicken with Mixed Vegetables & Pasta for a 9–12 month old.

Lunches are wonderful eaten outdoors and sometimes need to be on the run. You'll find recipes that work for you – Corn Fritters with Ham & Mango Salsa and Bean Dip Feast, for example – both perfect for filling lunchboxes or for picnics in the park or on the beach.

Wraps are fun, because you can fill them with your favourite foods and take them with you – to the park, the beach or wherever you're heading. Tahini is made of ground sesame seeds that contain a wealth of nutrients, including calcium and zinc, which are great for building little bones.

Chicken & Tahini Wrap

MAKES: 6
PREPARATION TIME: 30 minutes
COOKING TIME: 5 minutes
STORAGE: Refrigerate for up to 1 day.

....

3 tbsp extra virgin olive oil
3 boneless, skinless chicken breast fillets or 6 boneless, skinless chicken thigh fillets, cut into small strips
80g/2¾oz cauliflower, finely chopped
½ tbsp chopped sage leaves or ½ tsp dried sage
¾ tsp fine sea salt
¼ tsp freshly ground black pepper
6 tbsp tahini
6 wholemeal or multigrain tortilla wraps
3 carrots, grated
3 spring onions, white part only, finely sliced
½ lettuce, chopped
55g/2oz sprouts, such as alfalfa, broccoli or mung (optional)

1 Heat the oil in a large, heavy-based frying pan over a medium-high heat. Add the chicken and cauliflower and cook, stirring occasionally, for 4–5 minutes until the chicken is beginning to brown and is cooked through and the cauliflower is tender. Remove from the heat, add the sage, salt and pepper and mix well.

2 Spread 1 tablespoon of the tahini down the centre of each wrap and top with the cooked chicken and cauliflower, and the carrot, spring onions, lettuce and sprouts, if using. Roll up the wraps, tucking in one end, and serve.

(6-9) CHICKEN & CAULIFLOWER PURÉE
Put 4 tablespoons of the cooked chicken and cauliflower mixture and 3 tablespoons water in a blender. Blend for 30 seconds, adding extra water 1 teaspoon at a time, until smooth. Mix in 1 teaspoon of the oil and serve warm.

(9-12) CHICKEN WITH CAULIFLOWER, CARROTS & SPROUTS
Put 2 tablespoons of the cooked chicken, 1 tablespoon each of the cooked cauliflower, carrot and sprouts, if using, and 3 tablespoons water in a blender. Pulse for 15 seconds, adding extra water 1 teaspoon at a time, until the mixture forms a lumpy purée. Mix in 1 teaspoon of the oil and serve warm.

Burgers can be surprisingly healthy when you make
them at home with wholemeal buns, lettuce, tomato and
onion. You can also introduce wonderful extras such
as herbs on the inside and gherkins on the outside.

Chicken Burgers

SERVES: 2 adults, 1 child and 1 baby
PREPARATION TIME: 20 minutes
COOKING TIME: 10 minutes
STORAGE: Refrigerate for up to
1 day.

....

400g/14oz chicken mince, lamb
    mince, pork mince or beef mince
1 small onion, finely chopped,
    plus ½ onion, thinly sliced into
    rings, to serve
1 tsp chopped rosemary leaves
    (if using chicken mince)
½ tsp fine sea salt
¼ tsp freshly ground black pepper
2 tbsp extra virgin olive oil
mayonnaise, for spreading
3 wholemeal burger buns, halved
    horizontally
ketchup, for spreading
6 lettuce leaves
2 tomatoes, thinly sliced
3 gherkins, sliced lengthways

1 (6-9) (9-12) Put the chicken mince, onion, rosemary, salt and pepper in
a large bowl and mix well. Using your hands, shape the mixture into
3 burgers, using about twice the mixture for the adult portions that
you use for the child portion.

2 Heat the oil in a large, heavy-based frying pan over a medium heat.
Add the burgers to the pan and fry for 5 minutes on each side until lightly
browned and cooked through.

3 Spread mayonnaise on one half of each burger bun and ketchup
on the other and serve the burgers in the buns, topped with the onion
rings, lettuce, tomatoes and gherkins.

(6-9) **CHICKEN MINCE PURÉE**
Heat 1 teaspoon of the oil in a heavy-based frying pan over a medium
heat. Add 4 tablespoons of the chicken mince and fry, stirring occasionally,
for 3–4 minutes until the chicken is lightly browned and completely cooked
through. Transfer to a blender and add 3 tablespoons water. Blend for
30 seconds, adding extra water 1 teaspoon at a time, until smooth.
Serve warm.

(9-12) **CHICKEN & ONION MINCE**
Heat 1 teaspoon of the oil in a heavy-based frying pan over a medium heat.
Add 4 tablespoons of the chicken mince and 1 tablespoon of the chopped
onion and fry, stirring occasionally, for 3–4 minutes until the chicken is
lightly browned and completely cooked through. Transfer to a blender
and add 3 tablespoons water. Pulse for 15 seconds, adding extra water
1 teaspoon at a time, until the mixture forms a lumpy purée. Serve warm.

My brother, David, gave me this favourite recipe of his. The combination of chicken, ham and cheese create wonderful, strong flavours. My friend Kate made it and said it was so good that she managed to get her son Barny to eat cauliflower.

Chicken, Ham & Cheesy Pasta

SERVES: 2 adults, 1 child and 1 baby
PREPARATION TIME: 25 minutes
COOKING TIME: 30 minutes
STORAGE: Refrigerate for up to 1 day.

....

3 boneless, skinless chicken breast fillets or 6 boneless, skinless chicken thigh fillets
1 tbsp unsalted butter
85g/3oz cauliflower, cut into small florets
85g/3oz broccoli, cut into small florets
1 small green pepper, halved, deseeded and chopped
1 small onion, finely chopped
1 garlic clove, crushed
2 tbsp wholemeal spelt flour or wholemeal plain flour
85g/3oz ham, diced
30g/1oz mature Cheddar cheese, grated
30g/1oz Parmesan or Romano cheese, grated
1 tbsp Dijon mustard
1 tsp fine sea salt
300g/10½oz brown rice pasta, millet pasta, quinoa pasta or buckwheat pasta, any shape
freshly ground black pepper

1 Preheat the grill to medium. Put the chicken on a baking tray and grill for 5–8 minutes on each side until cooked through and the juices run clear. Remove from the grill and slice the chicken into thin slices. (6-9) (9-12)

2 Heat the butter in a large, heavy-based frying pan over a medium-high heat. Add the cauliflower, broccoli, pepper, onion and garlic and cook for 5 minutes until just cooked but crunchy. Stir in the flour, then add 185ml/6fl oz/¾ cup water and bring to the boil over a medium-high heat. Cook for about 5 minutes, stirring continuously, until the sauce thickens. Mix in the ham, cheeses, mustard and salt, and season with pepper.

3 Meanwhile, cook the pasta in plenty of boiling water, according to the packet instructions. Drain well, add to the cheesy sauce and mix well. Serve hot, topped with slices of chicken.

(6-9) CHICKEN, BROCCOLI & CAULIFLOWER PASTA PURÉE
Put 3 pieces each of the cauliflower and broccoli in a steamer and steam, covered, for 10 minutes until completely soft. Transfer to a blender and add 50g/1¾oz of the cooked chicken, 2 tablespoons of chopped, cooked pasta (without the cheesy sauce) and 4 tablespoons water. Blend for 30 seconds, adding extra water 1 teaspoon at a time, until smooth. Serve warm.

(9-12) CHICKEN WITH MIXED VEGETABLES & PASTA
Put 3 pieces each of the cauliflower and broccoli, 1 teaspoon of the onion and a pinch of the garlic in a steamer and steam, covered, for 10 minutes until completely soft. Transfer to a blender and add 50g/1¾oz of the cooked chicken, 2 tablespoons of chopped, cooked pasta (without the cheesy sauce) and 4 tablespoons water. Pulse for 15 seconds, adding extra water 1 teaspoon at a time, until the mixture forms a lumpy purée. Serve warm.

These fritters are good on their own, but with the mango salsa, they are incredible. We created them last summer when my sister, Jan, was here with her three kids, and her daughter Alli was asking for something to eat with the mango salsa I'd made.

Corn Fritters with Ham & Mango Salsa

MAKES: 12
PREPARATION TIME: 40 minutes
COOKING TIME: 30 minutes
STORAGE: Refrigerate the fritter batter for up to 1 day. Refrigerate the fritters and salsa for up to 3 days.

....

3 large eggs
180g/6¼oz/1½ cups wholemeal spelt flour or wholemeal plain flour
85g/3oz/heaped ½ cup fast-cook polenta
1½ tsp fine sea salt
5 tbsp extra virgin olive oil, plus extra for frying if needed
200g/7oz/1⅓ cups frozen sweetcorn, defrosted
300g/10½oz sliced ham
salad, to serve

FOR THE MANGO SALSA
2 ripe mangoes, peeled, pitted and chopped
200g/7oz cherry tomatoes
1 small red onion, finely chopped
4 tbsp lime juice

1 (6-9) (9-12) To make the salsa, put all of the ingredients in a blender and pulse for 15 seconds until chunky.

2 In a large mixing bowl, lightly beat the eggs together with a whisk. Add the flour, polenta, salt, 3 tablespoons of the oil and 185ml/6fl oz/¾ cup water and whisk. Add the sweetcorn and mix well.

3 Heat the remaining oil in a large, heavy-based frying pan over a medium-low heat. Working in batches, pour 2 tablespoons of the batter into the pan to make a fritter and repeat, spacing the fritters slightly apart. Cook for 4–5 minutes on each side or until lightly browned. Repeat with the remaining batter, adding more oil to the pan as needed. Top each fritter with sliced ham and a tablespoon of the salsa and serve warm with salad.

(6-9) **HAM & MANGO PURÉE**
Put 50g/1¾oz of the ham, 2 tablespoons of the mango and 3 tablespoons water in a blender. Blend for 30 seconds, adding extra water 1 teaspoon at a time, until smooth. Mix in 1 teaspoon of the oil and serve warm.

(9-12) **HAM, MANGO & RED ONION MIX**
Heat 1 teaspoon of the oil in a heavy-based frying pan over a low heat. Add 1 teaspoon of the onion and cook for 10 minutes until completely soft. Transfer to a blender and add 50g/1¾oz of the ham, 2 tablespoons of the mango and 3 tablespoons water. Pulse for 15 seconds, adding extra water 1 teaspoon at a time, until the mixture forms a lumpy purée. Serve warm.

This Creole mayonnaise is very quick to make and will jazz up any type of sandwich. Here I've put it with slices of steak – but you can also use leftover roast beef. My mother grew up in New Orleans, so she loves the Creole flavours in this.

Steak Sandwich with Creole Mayonnaise

SERVES: 2 adults, 1 child and 1 baby
PREPARATION TIME: 15 minutes
COOKING TIME: 8 minutes
STORAGE: Refrigerate the cooked steak for up to 1 day. Refrigerate the mayonnaise for up to 2 weeks.

. . . .

3 sirloin steaks
1 tbsp extra virgin olive oil
3 wholemeal rolls, halved horizontally
2 tomatoes, thinly sliced
6 Chinese leaves
¼ tsp fine sea salt

FOR THE CREOLE MAYONNAISE
125ml/4fl oz/½ cup mayonnaise
1 garlic clove, crushed
½ tsp Dijon mustard
¼ tsp hot pepper sauce
¾ tsp paprika
¼ tbsp fresh oregano or ¼ tsp dried oregano
½ tsp finely chopped thyme leaves or a large pinch of dried thyme

1 To make the mayonnaise, put all of the ingredients in a small bowl and mix thoroughly. (6-9) (9-12) Heat the oil in a frying pan over a medium heat. Season the steaks lightly with the salt and fry for 2–4 minutes on each side until they are cooked to your liking. Slice each steak into strips. Leave to cool, if you like.

2 Spread the mayonnaise generously over the roll halves. Serve the beef warm or cold in the buns, topped with the tomatoes and Chinese leaves.

(6-9) STEAK PURÉE
Put 50g/1¾oz of the steak and 1 teaspoon of the oil in a frying pan and cook for 10 minutes until the steak is browned and completely cooked through. Transfer to a blender and add 3 tablespoons water. Blend for 30 seconds, adding extra water 1 teaspoon at a time, until smooth. Serve warm.

(9-12) STEAK WITH CHINESE LEAF
Put 50g/1¾oz of the steak and 1 teaspoon of the oil in a frying pan and cook for 10 minutes until the steak is browned and completely cooked through. Transfer to a blender and add 1 Chinese leaf and 3 tablespoons water. Pulse for 15 seconds, adding extra water 1 teaspoon at a time, until the mixture forms a lumpy purée. Serve warm.

My sister Lauren said this is freakishly tasty and quick – and blew her mind. The Chinese flavours paired with nutty spelt or wholemeal pasta is a delightful surprise. If you have leftovers, the stir-fry is even tastier the next day over rice.

Chinese Five-Spice Pasta

SERVES: 2 adults, 1 child and 1 baby
PREPARATION TIME: 10 minutes
COOKING TIME: 10 minutes
STORAGE: Refrigerate for up to 1 day.

....

2 tbsp extra virgin olive oil
400g/14oz beef mince
300g/10½oz broccoli, chopped
2 tbsp tamari soy sauce or shoyu
   soy sauce
1 tsp Chinese five-spice
300g/10½oz wholemeal spelt conchiglie
   or wholemeal conchiglie
3 spring onions, green part only,
   finely sliced, to serve

1 Heat the oil in a large, heavy-based frying pan over a medium-high heat. Add the beef mince and broccoli and cook for 5–10 minutes until the broccoli is cooked but still crunchy and the beef mince has browned and cooked through. (6-9) (9-12) Add the tamari, Chinese five-spice and 4 tablespoons water and mix well.

2 Meanwhile, cook the pasta in plenty of boiling water, according to the packet instructions. Drain well, add to the beef and broccoli mixture and mix well. Serve hot, sprinkled with spring onions.

(6-9)

BEEF & BROCCOLI PURÉE
Heat a frying pan over a medium-low heat until hot. Add 4 tablespoons each of the cooked beef and cooked broccoli and 1 tablespoon water. Cook, stirring occasionally, for 10 minutes until the beef is completely cooked through and the broccoli is completely soft. Transfer to a blender and add 3 tablespoons water. Blend for 30 seconds, adding extra water 1 teaspoon at a time, until smooth. Serve warm.

(9-12)

BEEF, BROCCOLI & SPRING ONION
Heat a frying pan over a medium-low heat until hot. Add 4 tablespoons each of the cooked beef and cooked broccoli, 1 teaspoon of the spring onion and 1 tablespoon water. Cook, stirring occasionally, for 10 minutes until the beef is completely cooked through and the broccoli is completely soft. Transfer to a blender and add 3 tablespoons water. Pulse for 15 seconds, adding extra water 1 teaspoon at a time, until the mixture forms a lumpy purée. Serve warm.

Pretty and packed with flavour, this dish uses corn pasta because it's gluten-free and works for older babies. You can use any type of gluten-free pasta, such as rice, millet or quinoa. My kids like these vegetables, but I also make it with peas, broccoli and asparagus.

Prawn & Tri-Colour Vegetable Pasta

SERVES: 2 adults, 1 child and 1 baby
PREPARATION TIME: 15 minutes
COOKING TIME: 12 minutes
STORAGE: Refrigerate for up to 1 day.

....

1 carrot, halved lengthways and sliced
200g/7oz green beans, trimmed
    and halved
200g/7oz drained, bottled or tinned
    artichoke hearts in water or oil,
    chopped
3 tbsp extra virgin olive oil
2 garlic cloves, crushed
125ml/4fl oz/½ cup white wine
    or water
1 tbsp lemon juice
40g/1½oz butter
1 tsp fine sea salt
300g/10½oz cooked large king prawns
300g/10½oz corn pasta or gluten-free
    pasta, any shape

1 Put the carrot in a steamer and steam, covered, for 3 minutes. Add the green beans and steam, covered, for another 3 minutes until they are both cooked but still slightly crunchy. (6-9) (9-12) Transfer to a bowl, add the artichokes and mix well. Heat 2 tablespoons of the oil in a large, heavy-based frying pan over a medium heat. Add the garlic and cook for 1 minute, then pour in the wine and add the lemon juice, butter and salt. Bring to the boil over a high heat, then reduce the heat to medium and cook for 2 minutes. Add the prawns and cook for another 2 minutes until the prawns are hot.

2 Meanwhile, cook the pasta in plenty of boiling water, according to the packet instructions. Drain well and add to the vegetable mixture, then add the remaining oil and mix. Add the pasta and vegetables to the prawn mixture and stir well. Serve warm.

(6-9) GREEN BEAN, CARROT & ARTICHOKE PURÉE
Leave 3 tablespoons of the green beans and carrots in the steamer and steam, covered, for a further 20 minutes until completely soft. Transfer to a blender and add 2 tablespoons of the artichokes and 3 tablespoons water. Blend for 30 seconds, adding extra water 1 teaspoon at a time, until smooth. Mix in 1 teaspoon of the oil and serve warm.

(9-12) VEGETABLES WITH CORN PASTA
Leave 2 tablespoons of the green beans and carrots in the steamer and steam, covered, for a further 20 minutes until completely soft. Mix with 1 tablespoon of the artichokes and 2 tablespoons of chopped, cooked pasta (without the vegetable mixture and oil). Transfer to a blender and add 3 tablespoons water. Pulse for 15 seconds, adding extra water 1 teaspoon at a time, until the mixture forms a lumpy purée. Mix in 1 teaspoon of the oil and serve warm.

My children love sardines, but if yours don't, this is an excellent way to serve them as the fishy taste isn't too strong. These little fish are packed with omega-3 essential fats, so they're great for kids. Jessie loves these fishcakes so much that she asks for them every week and is learning to make them.

Sardine Fishcakes

MAKES: 10
PREPARATION TIME: 20 minutes
COOKING TIME: 30 minutes
STORAGE: Refrigerate for up to 1 day.

....

400g/14oz potatoes, diced
2 large eggs
180g/6¼oz tinned sardines in oil or
    water, drained
1 small onion, finely chopped
1 tbsp Dijon mustard
3 tbsp chopped parsley leaves
2 tsp finely grated lemon zest
a large pinch of cayenne pepper
½ tsp fine sea salt
75g/2½oz/¾ cup dried wholemeal
    breadcrumbs
1 tbsp extra virgin olive oil, plus extra
    for frying if needed
lemon wedges, to serve
salad, to serve

1 Put the potatoes in a steamer and steam, covered, for 10 minutes or until soft. Transfer to a large bowl and mash coarsely.

2 In a bowl, beat the eggs together with a whisk. (6-9) (9-12) In another bowl, mash the sardines with a fork. Add the eggs, onion, mustard, parsley, lemon zest, cayenne pepper, salt and breadcrumbs and mix well. Add to the mashed potatoes and mix until well combined. Using your hands, divide the mixture into 10 equal pieces and shape each one into a fishcake.

3 Heat the oil in a large, heavy-based frying pan over a medium-low heat. Working in batches, carefully add the fishcakes to the pan and cook for 3 minutes on each side until browned and heated through. Repeat with the remaining fishcakes, adding more oil to the pan as needed. Serve warm with lemon wedges and salad.

(6-9) SARDINE PURÉE
Put 4 sardines and 3 tablespoons water in a blender. Blend for 30 seconds, adding extra water 1 teaspoon at a time, until smooth. Serve warm.

(9-12) SARDINE, ONION & PARSLEY MIX
Heat 1 teaspoon of the oil in a heavy-based frying pan over a low heat. Add 1 teaspoon of the onion and cook for 10 minutes until completely soft. Transfer to a blender and add 4 sardines, 1 teaspoon of the parsley and 3 tablespoons water. Pulse for 15 seconds, adding extra water 1 teaspoon at a time, until the mixture forms a lumpy purée. Serve warm.

This is easy, delicious and very versatile. For a vegetarian version, you can make it without the mackerel and simply top the cooked vegetables with a dollop of bean dip (see page 68). You can change the vegetables, too. I like potato as the base, but you might like sweet potato, spinach or broad beans.

Mackerel on Veg

SERVES: 2 adults, 1 child and 1 baby
PREPARATION TIME: 20 minutes
COOKING TIME: 20 minutes
STORAGE: Refrigerate for up to 1 day.

....

300g/10½oz potatoes, diced
200g/7oz squash, deseeded and cut into chunks, or pumpkin, peeled, deseeded and cut into chunks
1 small carrot, chopped
1 small leek, chopped
10 garlic cloves
75g/2½oz broccoli, cut into small florets
75g/2½oz green beans, trimmed and halved
400g/14oz mackerel fillets
extra virgin olive oil, to serve

1 (6-9) (9-12) Put the potatoes, squash, carrot, leek and garlic in a steamer and steam, covered, for 12–15 minutes. Add the broccoli and green beans, put the mackerel on top of the vegetables and steam, covered, for another 5 minutes until the vegetables are tender and the mackerel is cooked through. Serve warm with extra virgin olive oil.

(6-9) **MACKEREL & VEGETABLE PURÉE**
Put 2 squash pieces in a steamer and steam, covered, for 10 minutes. Add 1 tablespoon of the carrot and steam, covered, for a further 10 minutes. Add 3 pieces each of the broccoli and green beans and steam, covered, for another 10 minutes until the vegetables are completely soft. Remove the skin and any bones from 50g/1¾oz of the steamed mackerel. Transfer to a blender and add the steamed vegetables and 3 tablespoons water. Blend for 30 seconds, adding extra water 1 teaspoon at a time, until smooth. Mix in 1 teaspoon of the oil and serve warm.

(9-12) **MACKEREL & VEGETABLE MEDLEY**
Put 2 squash pieces in a steamer and steam, covered, for 10 minutes. Add 1 tablespoon of the carrot and steam, covered, for a further 10 minutes. Add 1 of the garlic cloves, 2 leek pieces and 3 pieces each of the broccoli and green beans and steam, covered, for another 10 minutes until the vegetables are completely soft. Remove the skin and any bones from 50g/1¾oz of the steamed mackerel, then transfer to a bowl and mash with a fork. Transfer to a blender and add the steamed vegetables and 3 tablespoons water. Pulse for 15 seconds, adding extra water 1 teaspoon at a time, until the mixture forms a lumpy purée. Mix in 1 teaspoon of the oil and serve warm with the mashed mackerel.

My mom sometimes makes this cauliflower for us the day we fly home to see her and my dad over the Christmas holidays. It's a light snack to tide us over until dinner after the long flight. I've added salmon for a great lunch and if you serve it with a little rice, pasta or bread, you have a complete meal.

Baked Salmon, Cauli & Capers

SERVES: 2 adults, 1 child and 1 baby
PREPARATION TIME: 20 minutes, plus at least 7 hours soaking and 40 minutes cooking the brown rice
COOKING TIME: 20 minutes
STORAGE: Refrigerate for up to 1 day.

....

6 tbsp extra virgin olive oil
3 salmon steaks
1 cauliflower, sliced into rounds
¼ tsp fine sea salt
1 red onion, thinly sliced into rings
4 tbsp small capers in salt or brine, drained and rinsed
3 garlic cloves, finely chopped
4 tbsp chopped parsley leaves
freshly ground black pepper
1 recipe quantity cooked brown rice (see page 23), to serve

1 (6-9) (9-12) Preheat the oven to 200°C/400°F/gas 6 and grease a large baking tray with 2 tablespoons of the oil. Arrange the salmon and cauliflower in a single layer on the bottom of the baking tray and drizzle the remaining oil over the top. Sprinkle with the salt and season with pepper. Top each salmon steak with ⅓ of the onion rings.

2 Bake for 15–20 minutes until the cauliflower is tender and browned around the edges and the salmon is opaque and cooked through. Serve hot with the capers, garlic and parsley sprinkled over the top, and with the cooked brown rice.

(6-9) **SALMON & CAULIFLOWER PURÉE**
Remove the skin and any bones from 50g/1¾oz of the salmon. Transfer to a greased baking dish, add 6 cauliflower florets and bake as above for 20 minutes until the salmon is opaque and completely cooked through and the cauliflower is completely soft. Transfer to a blender and add 3 tablespoons water. Blend for 30 seconds, adding extra water 1 teaspoon at a time, until smooth. Serve warm.

 BAKED SALMON & VEGETABLES
Remove the skin and any bones from 50g/1¾oz of the salmon. Transfer to a greased baking dish, add 6 cauliflower florets and 1 onion ring and bake as above for 20 minutes until the salmon is opaque and completely cooked through and the vegetables are completely soft. Transfer to a blender and add 3 tablespoons water. Pulse for 15 seconds, adding extra water 1 teaspoon at a time, until the mixture forms a lumpy purée. Serve warm.

My sister Lauren thinks this is a phenomenal recipe. I know she loves the flavours – and I love the fabulous ingredients like broad beans, sprouts, beetroot and toasted seeds. It's a beautiful salad – and filling enough to be a meal.

Dreamy Salad with Squash

SERVES: 2 adults, 1 child and 1 baby
PREPARATION TIME: 30 minutes
COOKING TIME: 25 minutes
STORAGE: Use the same day.

....

1 butternut squash, deseeded and
    cut into bite-sized pieces
6 tbsp extra virgin olive oil
½ tsp fine sea salt
100g/3½oz shelled broad beans
3 tbsp pumpkin seeds
3 tbsp sunflower seeds
1 tbsp tamari soy sauce or shoyu
    soy sauce
100g/3½oz feta cheese, cut into
    bite-sized pieces
¼ lettuce, such as romaine or batavia,
    washed and chopped
1 avocado, peeled, pitted and cut
    into bite-sized pieces
1 beetroot, grated
1 tbsp balsamic vinegar
50g/1¾oz sprouts, such as alfalfa,
    broccoli or mung (optional)
freshly ground black pepper

1 Preheat the grill to medium. Put the squash in a baking dish with 2 tablespoons of the oil and toss well. Grill for 20 minutes until tender. Remove from the grill, sprinkle the salt over the top and season with pepper. Meanwhile, put the the broad beans in a steamer and steam, covered, for 3–4 minutes until they are cooked but still retain a slight bite.

2 Heat a large frying pan over a medium-low heat. Mix together the seeds and tamari in a small bowl. Add the seed mix to the pan and cook, stirring with a wooden spoon, for 3–5 minutes until the pan is dry and the seeds are lightly browned.

3 Put the grilled squash, steamed broad beans, toasted seeds, feta, lettuce, avocado, beetroot, balsamic vinegar, sprouts, if using, and the remaining oil in a large bowl. Toss well and serve.

6-9 SQUASH, BROAD BEAN & AVOCADO PURÉE
Put 2 tablespoons of the grilled squash, 1 tablespoon of the steamed broad beans, 2 tablespoons of the avocado and 3 tablespoons water in a blender. Blend for 30 seconds, adding extra water 1 teaspoon at a time, until smooth. Serve warm.

 SQUASH, BROAD BEAN & AVOCADO
WITH BEETROOT & SPROUTS
Put 2 tablespoons of the grilled squash, 1 tablespoon each of the steamed broad beans, avocado, beetroot and sprouts, if using, and 3 tablespoons water in a blender. Pulse for 15 seconds, adding extra water 1 teaspoon at a time, until the mixture forms a lumpy purée. Serve warm.

I first tried spelt salad in Tuscany. Friends nearby invited us to a picnic on a roasting hot summer day near a freezing mountain stream. After we had all cooled off, we shared out the food we had brought. Our friend Susanna offered spelt salad for us to try, which is a classic dish in the region.

Tuscan Spelt Salad

SERVES: 2 adults, 1 child and 1 baby
PREPARATION TIME: 20 minutes, plus at least 7 hours soaking (optional)
COOKING TIME: 35–45 minutes
STORAGE: Refrigerate for up to 3 days.

....

150g/5½oz/¾ cup wholemeal spelt grain
¾ tbsp natural yogurt or kefir, for soaking (optional)
1 tsp fine sea salt
4 tbsp extra virgin olive oil
2 tbsp white wine vinegar
250g/9oz mozzarella cheese, diced
1 large tomato, chopped
1 courgette, quartered lengthways and sliced
1 fennel bulb, chopped
1 small red onion, finely chopped
1 small garlic clove, finely chopped
3 tbsp chopped parsley leaves
2 tbsp finely chopped mint leaves

1 If soaking the spelt grain, put the spelt grain and yogurt in a large saucepan and cover generously with warm water. Leave to soak, covered, for 7 hours or overnight at room temperature. Drain and rinse the grains, then return to the pan and add 375ml/13fl oz/1½ cups water.

2 Bring to the boil over a high heat. Turn the heat down to low and simmer, covered, for 30–35 minutes, stirring occasionally, until the grains are tender but not mushy. Drain and transfer to a large bowl.

(If cooking unsoaked spelt grain, put the spelt grain and 455ml/16fl oz/ scant 2 cups water in a large saucepan. Bring to the boil over a high heat. Turn the heat down to low and simmer, covered, for 45 minutes, stirring occasionally, until the grains are tender but not mushy. Drain and transfer to a large bowl.)

3 (6-9) (9-12) Add the salt, oil and white wine vinegar and mix well. Leave to cool slightly, then add all of the remaining ingredients and mix well. Serve either warm or cold.

(6-9)

COURGETTE PURÉE
Put ½ of the sliced courgette in a steamer and steam, covered, for 10 minutes until completely soft. Transfer to a blender and add 2 tablespoons water. Blend for 30 seconds, adding extra water 1 teaspoon at a time, until smooth. Mix in 1 teaspoon of the oil and serve warm.

(9-12)

COURGETTE, FENNEL, RED ONION & HERB MIX
Put ½ of the sliced courgette, 1 tablespoon of the fennel and 1 teaspoon of the onion in a steamer and steam, covered, for 10 minutes until completely soft. Transfer to a blender and add a pinch each of the parsley and mint leaves and 2 tablespoons water. Pulse for 15 seconds, adding extra water 1 teaspoon at a time, until the mixture forms a lumpy purée. Mix in 1 teaspoon of the oil and serve warm.

I love a well-made mushroom soup. In this one, the flavours are deepened by the dried porcini or shiitake mushrooms and by browning off the mushrooms first. Half-puréeing the soup gives a great texture, leaving chunks of mushroom, leek and parsley.

Simple Mushroom Soup

SERVES: 2 adults, 1 child and 1 baby
PREPARATION TIME: 30 minutes, plus at least 7 hours soaking and 20 minutes cooking the buckwheat
COOKING TIME: 55 minutes
STORAGE: Refrigerate for up to 3 days, or freeze for up to 3 months.

....

30g/1oz dried porcini or shiitake mushrooms
4 tbsp extra virgin olive oil, plus extra to serve
1 leek, halved lengthways and sliced
450g/1lb button mushrooms, sliced
1 recipe quantity cooked buckwheat (see page 22)
2 tsp finely chopped thyme leaves
2½ tsp fine sea salt
4 tbsp chopped parsley leaves
wholemeal bread, to serve

1 Soak the porcini mushrooms in 240ml/8fl oz/scant 1 cup boiling water for 10 minutes until softened. Drain, squeeze out any excess water and chop.

2 (6-9) (9-12) Heat the oil in a large, heavy-based frying pan over a medium-high heat. Add the leek and cook, stirring occasionally, for 10 minutes until soft. Add the porcini and button mushrooms and cook for 10 minutes until the mushrooms are beginning to brown.

3 Pour 750ml/26fl oz/3 cups boiling water into a large, heavy-based saucepan and stir in the mushroom and leek mixture, cooked buckwheat, thyme and salt. Bring to the boil over a high heat, then turn the heat down to low and simmer, covered, for 35 minutes.

4 Add the parsley, then transfer ½ of the soup to a blender and blend until smooth. Return the blended soup to the pan, reheating if necessary. Serve hot with extra oil and wholemeal bread.

 BUCKWHEAT PURÉE
Put 4 tablespoons of the cooked buckwheat and 135ml/4½fl oz/generous ½ cup water in a saucepan and simmer, covered, over a low heat for 20 minutes until completely soft. Transfer to a blender and add 2 tablespoons water. Blend for 30 seconds, adding extra water 1 teaspoon at a time, until smooth. Mix in 1 teaspoon of the oil and serve warm.

 BUCKWHEAT & LEEK MIX
Put 4 tablespoons of the cooked buckwheat and 135ml/4½fl oz/generous ½ cup water in a saucepan and simmer, covered, over a low heat for 20 minutes until completely soft. Transfer to a blender and add 2 tablespoons of the cooked leek and 2 tablespoons water. Pulse for 15 seconds, adding extra water 1 teaspoon at a time, until the mixture forms a lumpy purée. Mix in 1 teaspoon of the oil and serve warm.

We love hummus, but prefer this dip because of the dreamy creaminess created by the cannellini beans (my brother David's suggestion). When Cassie sees me putting beans in the blender she exclaims, 'hummy' with glee. We eat it by the bowlful with toppings and veg.

Bean Dip Feast

SERVES: 2 adults, 1 child and 1 baby
PREPARATION TIME: 20 minutes, plus at least 12 hours soaking and 1 hour 10 minutes cooking the cannellini beans (optional), and at least 12 hours soaking and 2 hours 10 minutes cooking the chickpeas (optional)
COOKING TIME: 5 minutes
STORAGE: Refrigerate the dip for up to 3 days.

....

55g/2oz/heaped ⅓ cup pine nuts
3 tbsp extra virgin olive oil
3 tbsp chopped parsley leaves
3 pinches of paprika
2 carrots, cut into rounds, to serve
1 cucumber, cut into rounds, to serve
1 small yellow pepper, halved, deseeded, and cut into chunks, to serve
1 endive, leaves separated, to serve
wholemeal pitta breads, to serve

FOR THE BEAN DIP
1 recipe quantity cooked dried cannellini beans (see page 23) or 270g/9½oz/ 1½ cups drained, tinned cannellini beans, rinsed
1 recipe quantity cooked dried chickpeas (see page 24) or 220g/7¾oz/1⅓ cups drained, tinned chickpeas, rinsed
3 tbsp lemon juice
6 tbsp extra virgin olive oil
2 garlic cloves, crushed
2 tsp fine sea salt
6 tbsp tahini

1 Preheat the grill to medium. Put the pine nuts on a baking tray and toast under the grill for 3–5 minutes until beginning to brown.

2 (6-9) (9-12) To make the bean dip, put the cooked cannellini beans and cooked chickpeas in a food processor or blender. (Add the kombu, if used during cooking.) Add the lemon juice, oil, garlic, salt and 200ml/7fl oz/ scant 1 cup water and blend for 1 minute until smooth. Add the tahini and mix well.

3 Spoon 6 tablespoons of the dip into three bowls and drizzle each with 1 tablespoon of the oil. Sprinkle 1 tablespoon of the toasted pine nuts, 1 tablespoon of the parsley and a pinch of paprika over the top of each bowl. Serve with the carrots, cucumber, pepper, endive leaves and wholemeal pitta breads.

(6-9) **CANNELLINI & CHICKPEA PURÉE**
Put 2 tablespoons each of the cooked cannellini beans and cooked chickpeas and 2 tablespoons water in a blender. Blend for 30 seconds, adding extra water 1 teaspoon at a time, until smooth. Mix in 1 teaspoon of the oil and serve warm.

(9-12) **CANNELLINI & CHICKPEAS WITH CUCUMBER**
Put 2 tablespoons each of the cooked cannellini beans and cooked chickpeas, 4 cucumber pieces and 1 tablespoon water in a blender. Pulse for 15 seconds, adding extra water 1 teaspoon at a time, until the mixture forms a lumpy purée. Mix in 1 teaspoon of the oil and serve warm.

Eggs are the perfect protein and if you mix them with a load of vegetables and some rice, you get a brilliantly simple meal that is quick but nourishing.

Rainbow Veg & Rice Omelette

SERVES: 2 adults, 1 child and 1 baby
PREPARATION TIME: 10 minutes, plus at least 7 hours soaking and 40 minutes cooking the brown rice
COOKING TIME: 16 minutes
STORAGE: Refrigerate for up to 1 day.

....

6 large eggs
½ tsp fine sea salt
¼ tsp hot pepper sauce
3 tbsp extra virgin olive oil
100g/3½oz asparagus, woody ends removed and stalks chopped
1 small red pepper, halved, deseeded and diced
100g/3½oz mushrooms, sliced
1 small onion, finely chopped
1 small courgette, grated
1 carrot, grated
2 garlic cloves, finely chopped
½ recipe quantity cooked brown rice (see page 23)

1 In a bowl, lightly beat the eggs together with a whisk. Add the salt and hot pepper sauce and whisk. Heat 2 tablespoons of the oil in a large, heavy-based frying pan over a medium-high heat. (9-12) Add the asparagus, pepper, mushrooms and onion and cook, stirring occasionally, for 5 minutes. (6-9) Add the courgette, carrot, garlic and cooked brown rice, and cook for a further 3 minutes until any juice from the vegetables has evaporated, the rice has warmed through and the vegetables are beginning to brown.

2 Transfer the vegetable and rice mixture to a bowl. Reduce the heat to medium and add the remaining oil to the pan, tilting the pan to evenly coat the base. Add the eggs and cook for 4–5 minutes until the eggs are just beginning to set, then spoon the rice and vegetable mixture evenly over the top. Cover partially with a lid and cook for another 3 minutes until the omelette is just cooked through and browned and crisp on the bottom. Serve hot.

(6-9) **BROWN RICE, COURGETTE & CARROT PURÉE**
Put 4 tablespoons of the cooked brown rice, 1 tablespoon each of the courgette and carrot and 135ml/4½fl oz/generous ½ cup boiling water in a saucepan and simmer, covered, over a low heat for 20 minutes until completely soft. Transfer to a blender and blend for 30 seconds, adding water 1 teaspoon at a time, until smooth. Mix in 1 teaspoon of the oil and serve warm.

(9-12) **BROWN RICE WITH ASPARAGUS, COURGETTE & CARROT**
Put 4 tablespoons of the cooked brown rice and 135ml/4½fl oz/generous ½ cup boiling water in a saucepan and simmer, covered, over a low heat for 10 minutes. Add 3 asparagus pieces and simmer for a further 10 minutes until completely soft. Remove from the heat and mix in 1 tablespoon each of the courgette and carrot. Transfer to a blender and pulse for 15 seconds, adding water 1 teaspoon at a time, until the mixture forms a lumpy purée. Mix in 1 teaspoon of the oil and serve warm.

To my horror, my friend Kate told me that she doesn't like quinoa. What's not to like? I met the challenge with a plea for her to make these tomatoes at home. She did, said it's a great recipe and is now a convert.

Quinoa-Stuffed Tomatoes

SERVES: 2 adults, 1 child and 1 baby
PREPARATION TIME: 20 minutes, plus at least 7 hours soaking and 20 minutes cooking the quinoa
COOKING TIME: 35 minutes
STORAGE: Refrigerate for up to 3 days.

....

50g/1¾oz/⅓ cup pine nuts
2 tbsp extra virgin olive oil, plus extra
    for greasing
1 leek, quartered lengthways and sliced
½ recipe quantity cooked quinoa
    (see page 22)
80g/2¾oz Parmesan cheese, grated
1 garlic clove, crushed
½ tsp fine sea salt
3 large tomatoes
salad, to serve

1 Preheat the grill to medium. Put the pine nuts on a baking tray and toast under the grill for 3 minutes until lightly browned.

2 Preheat the oven to 160°C/315°F/gas 2–3 and grease a large baking dish with oil. (6-9) (9-12) Heat the oil in a heavy-based saucepan over a medium heat. Add the leek and cook, stirring occasionally, for 10 minutes until soft.

3 Mix the toasted pine nuts, cooked leek, cooked quinoa, Parmesan, garlic and salt in a small bowl. Cut the tomatoes in half horizontally, then scoop out and discard the flesh and seeds. Spoon the quinoa mixture into each tomato half until filled to the top. Put the stuffed tomatoes in the baking dish and bake for 20 minutes until the cheese has melted and is beginning to brown. Serve hot with salad.

(6-9)

QUINOA PURÉE
Put 4 tablespoons of the cooked quinoa and 135ml/4½fl oz/generous ½ cup boiling water in a saucepan and simmer, covered, over a low heat for 20 minutes until completely soft. Transfer to a blender and add 2 tablespoons water. Blend for 30 seconds, adding extra water 1 teaspoon at a time, until smooth. Mix in 1 teaspoon of the oil and serve warm.

(9-12)

QUINOA WITH LEEKS
Put 4 tablespoons of the cooked quinoa and 135ml/4½fl oz/generous ½ cup boiling water in a saucepan and simmer, covered, over a low heat for 20 minutes until completely soft. Transfer to a blender and add 1 tablespoon of the cooked leeks and 2 tablespoons water. Pulse for 15 seconds, adding extra water 1 teaspoon at a time, until the mixture forms a lumpy purée. Mix in 1 teaspoon of the oil and serve warm.

Wild rice is a great food that many people either don't know about or forget about. It has a wonderfully chewy texture and a slight nutty flavour. You can also use other types of rice or pasta when you feel like a change.

Wild Rice Pancakes

MAKES: 12
PREPARATION TIME: 15 minutes, plus at least 7 hours soaking and 40 minutes cooking the wild rice
COOKING TIME: 18 minutes
STORAGE: Refrigerate for up to 3 days.

....

2 large eggs
60g/2¼oz/½ cup wholemeal spelt flour or wholemeal plain flour
1 recipe quantity cooked wild rice (see page 23)
2 tbsp natural yogurt
100g/3½oz fresh or defrosted, frozen baby spinach leaves, finely chopped
100g/3½oz feta cheese, diced
¾ tsp fine sea salt
½ tsp cayenne pepper
1 tbsp extra virgin olive oil, plus extra for frying if needed
salad, to serve

1 Put the eggs and 2 tablespoons water in a large mixing bowl and lightly beat together with a whisk. (6-9) (9-12) Whisk in the flour, then add the cooked wild rice, yogurt, spinach, feta, salt and cayenne pepper and mix well.

2 Heat the oil in a large, heavy-based frying pan over a medium heat. Working in batches, pour 2 tablespoons of the batter into the pan to make a pancake and repeat, spacing the pancakes slightly apart. Cook for 3 minutes on each side or until lightly browned. Repeat with the remaining batter, adding more oil to the pan as needed. Serve warm with salad.

(6-9) **WILD RICE PURÉE**
Put 4 tablespoons of the cooked wild rice and 150ml/5fl oz/scant ⅔ cup boiling water in a saucepan and simmer, covered, over a low heat for 20 minutes until completely soft. Transfer the rice to a blender and add 2 tablespoons water. Blend for 30 seconds, adding extra water 1 teaspoon at a time, until smooth. Mix in 1 teaspoon of the oil and serve warm.

(9-12) **WILD RICE WITH YOGURT**
Put 4 tablespoons of the cooked wild rice and 150ml/5fl oz/scant ⅔ cup boiling water in a saucepan and simmer, covered, over a low heat for 20 minutes until completely soft. Transfer the rice to a blender and add 2 tablespoons of the yogurt and 1 tablespoon water. Pulse for 15 seconds, adding extra water 1 teaspoon at a time, until the mixture forms a lumpy purée. Mix in 1 teaspoon of the oil and serve warm.

Fried Root Rosti
with Poached Eggs

MAKES: 6
PREPARATION TIME: 20 minutes,
plus 7 hours soaking and 40
minutes cooking the brown rice
COOKING TIME: 25 minutes
STORAGE: Refrigerate the
uncooked rosti mixture for up
to 1 day.

....

7 large eggs
1 large sweet potato, grated
1 small swede or 2 parsnips, peeled
    and grated
½ recipe quantity cooked brown
    rice (see page 23)
4 tbsp wholemeal spelt flour
    or wholemeal plain flour
1 tbsp wholegrain mustard
1 tsp fine sea salt
2 tbsp extra virgin olive oil, plus
    extra for frying if needed
1 tbsp white wine vinegar
    or grape vinegar
freshly ground black pepper
salad, to serve

1 Preheat the oven to 100°C/200°F/gas ½. In a large mixing bowl, lightly beat 1 of the eggs with a whisk. (6-9) (9-12) Add the sweet potato, swede, cooked brown rice, flour, mustard and salt and mix well.

2 Heat the oil in a large, heavy-based frying pan over a medium-high heat. Working in batches, scoop 4 tablespoons of the mixture into your hand and shape it into a rosti. Using the back of a metal spoon, flatten the top and and smooth the sides. Flip your hand over so the rosti lands in the pan and flatten the top with a spatula. Fry for 4–5 minutes on each side until golden brown. Repeat with the remaining mixture, adding more oil to the pan as needed. Keep the rostis warm in the oven while you poach the eggs.

3 Bring a large saucepan of water to the boil, then turn the heat down to low. Add the vinegar, then crack 1 egg into the gently simmering water. Repeat with the remaining 5 eggs and simmer for 3 minutes. Remove the eggs from the pan, using a slotted spoon, and drain on a plate lined with kitchen paper. Top each rosti with a poached egg, season with freshly ground black pepper and serve warm with salad.

(6-9)

SWEET POTATO, SWEDE & RICE PURÉE
Put 1 tablespoon each of the sweet potato and swede, 4 tablespoons of the cooked brown rice, 1 teaspoon of the oil and 135ml/4½fl oz/generous ½ cup water in a heavy-based frying pan. Cook, covered, over a low heat for 20 minutes until completely soft. Transfer to a blender and add 3 tablespoons water. Blend for 30 seconds, adding extra water 1 teaspoon at a time, until smooth. Serve warm.

(9-12)

SWEDE & BROWN RICE WITH SWEET POTATO
Put 2 tablespoons of the swede, 4 tablespoons of the cooked brown rice, 1 teaspoon of the oil and 135ml/4½fl oz/generous ½ cup water in a heavy-based frying pan. Cook, covered, over a low heat for 20 minutes until completely soft. Transfer to a blender and add 2 tablespoons of the sweet potato and 3 tablespoons water. Pulse for 15 seconds, adding extra water 1 teaspoon at a time, until the mixture forms a lumpy purée. Serve warm.

I offered this lunch recipe to my friend Julia who made it with some hesitation. However, she came back with rave reviews, remarking on the wonderfully lively flavours of lime juice, cumin and coriander – and thinks it's a perfect summer dish.

Spiced Red Beans with Corn & Rice

SERVES: 2 adults, 1 child and 1 baby
PREPARATION TIME: 25 minutes, plus 1 hour standing, plus at least 12 hours soaking and 1 hour 40 minutes cooking the kidney beans (optional), plus 1 hour standing, plus at least 7 hours soaking and 40 minutes cooking the brown rice
COOKING TIME: 4 minutes
STORAGE: Refrigerate for up to 3 days.

....

165g/5¾oz/heaped 1 cup frozen sweetcorn
1 recipe quantity cooked dried kidney beans (see page 24) or 500g/1lb 2oz/2½ cups drained tinned kidney beans, rinsed
1 orange pepper, deseeded and diced
1 small red onion, finely chopped
1 garlic clove, finely chopped
5 tbsp extra virgin olive oil
4 tbsp lime juice
1 tsp ground cumin
2 tsp fine sea salt
1 recipe quantity cooked brown rice (see page 23)
8 tbsp chopped coriander leaves

1 Put the sweetcorn in a steamer and steam, covered, for 3–4 minutes until just tender.

2 (6-9) (9-12) Put the cooked kidney beans in a large bowl. (Chop and add the kombu, if used during cooking.) Add the sweetcorn, pepper, onion, garlic, oil, lime juice, cumin and ½ of the salt and mix well. Cover and leave to stand at room temperature for at least 1 hour.

3 Put the cooked brown rice in a large bowl, add the remaining salt and mix well. Mix the coriander into the bean mixture and serve over the warm rice.

(6-9) **RED BEAN & BROWN RICE PURÉE**
Put 4 tablespoons of the cooked brown rice and 135ml/4½fl oz/generous ½ cup boiling water in a saucepan and simmer, covered, over a low heat for 20 minutes until completely soft. Transfer to a blender and add 2 tablespoons of the cooked kidney beans and 3 tablespoons water. Blend for 30 seconds, adding extra water 1 teaspoon at a time, until smooth. Mix in 1 teaspoon of the oil and serve warm.

(9-12) **SPICED RED BEANS & RICE**
Put 4 tablespoons of the cooked brown rice, ½ teaspoon each of the onion and coriander and 135ml/4½fl oz/generous ½ cup boiling water in a saucepan and simmer, covered, over a low heat for 20 minutes until completely soft. Transfer to a blender and add 2 tablespoons of the cooked kidney beans and 3 tablespoons water. Pulse for 15 seconds, adding extra water 1 teaspoon at a time, until the mixture forms a lumpy purée. Mix in 1 teaspoon of the oil and serve warm.

This simple yet delicious vegetable pasta makes a great lunch. It's a favourite of Jessie's because she loves artichokes and peas, and anything with lemon – which in this dish lifts and brightens the Parmesan cheese.

Corn Pasta with Artichoke & Peas

SERVES: 2 adults, 1 child and 1 baby
PREPARATION TIME: 20 minutes
COOKING TIME: 12 minutes
STORAGE: Refrigerate for up to 3 days.

....

5 tbsp extra virgin olive oil
1 onion, chopped
3 garlic cloves, finely chopped
450g/1lb drained, bottled or tinned artichoke hearts in water or oil, chopped
185g/6½oz/1¼ cups defrosted, frozen peas or fresh, podded peas
40g/1½oz Parmesan cheese, grated
2 tbsp lemon juice
300g/10½oz corn or gluten-free pasta
½ tsp fine sea salt

1 (6-9) Heat 2 tablespoons of the oil in a large, heavy-based frying pan over a medium heat. Add the onion and cook, stirring occasionally, for 5 minutes until beginning to brown, then turn the heat up to medium-high. Add the garlic and artichokes and cook, stirring occasionally, for a further 5 minutes until lightly browned. Add the peas and cook for 2 minutes until heated through. (9-12) Transfer to a large bowl, add the Parmesan, lemon juice and 1 tablespoon of the oil and mix well.

2 Meanwhile, cook the pasta in plenty of boiling water, according to the packet instructions. Drain well, then mix in the salt and the remaining oil. Add the pasta to the artichoke mixture and mix well. Serve warm.

(6-9)

ARTICHOKE & PEA PURÉE
Heat 1 teaspoon of the oil and 3 tablespoons water in a frying pan over a low heat. Add 3 tablespoons of the peas and cook, covered, for 10 minutes until completely soft. Add 9 artichoke pieces and cook for a further 2–3 minutes until the artichoke has warmed through. Transfer to a blender and add 3 tablespoons water. Blend for 30 seconds, adding extra water 1 teaspoon at a time, until smooth. Serve warm.

(9-12)

CORN PASTA, ARTICHOKE & PEA
Put 3 tablespoons of the cooked artichoke and pea mixture, 2 tablespoons of chopped, cooked corn pasta (without the salt or oil) and 3 tablespoons water in a blender. Pulse for 15 seconds, adding extra water 1 teaspoon at a time, until the mixture forms a lumpy purée. Mix in 1 teaspoon of the oil and serve warm.

Tofu, when marinated, takes on lots of flavour, so it's great with this fabulous marinade. Toasted sesame oil, which is used here, is a wonderful condiment to keep in your kitchen, and tofu can be added to any stir-fry recipe to provide extra protein.

Marinated Tofu Stir-Fry

SERVES: 2 adults, 1 child and 1 baby
PREPARATION TIME: 25 minutes, plus 30 minutes marinating, plus at least 7 hours soaking and 40 minutes cooking the brown rice
COOKING TIME: 15 minutes
STORAGE: Refrigerate for up to 3 days.

....

250g/9oz tofu, patted dry and cut into bite-sized pieces
2 tbsp sesame seeds
2 tbsp toasted sesame oil
250g/9oz broccoli, cut into bite-sized florets
200g/7oz mangetout, trimmed and halved
1½ recipe quantities cooked brown rice (see page 23), to serve

FOR THE MARINADE
2 tbsp lemon juice
4 tsp grated root ginger
2 garlic cloves, crushed
3 tbsp tamari soy sauce or shoyu soy sauce
2 tbsp toasted sesame oil

1 (9-12) To make the marinade, put all of the ingredients in a non-reactive bowl and mix well. Add the tofu and stir well, making sure the tofu is covered in the marinade. Cover and leave to marinate at room temperature for 30 minutes.

2 Meanwhile, toast the sesame seeds in a dry frying pan over a medium heat for 1–2 minutes, stirring occasionally, until golden.

3 Heat the oil in a wok or large frying pan over a medium heat. Add the tofu to the pan and reserve any remaining marinade. (6-9) Stir-fry for 5 minutes until beginning to brown, then add the broccoli, mangetout, the remaining marinade and 125ml/4fl oz/½ cup hot water and stir-fry, stirring, for another 5 minutes until the vegetables are soft. Serve hot over the cooked brown rice, with the toasted sesame seeds sprinkled over the top.

(6-9) MANGETOUT, BROCCOLI & BROWN RICE PURÉE
Put 4 tablespoons of the cooked brown rice and 135ml/4½fl oz/generous ½ cup boiling water in a saucepan and simmer, covered, over a low heat for 10 minutes. Add 6 pieces each of the mangetout and broccoli and simmer, covered, for a further 10 minutes until completely soft. Transfer to a blender and add 3 tablespoons water. Blend for 30 seconds, adding extra water 1 teaspoon at a time, until smooth. Serve warm.

(9-12) MANGETOUT, BROCCOLI, GARLIC & BROWN RICE
Put 4 tablespoons of the cooked brown rice and 135ml/4½fl oz/generous ½ cup boiling water in a saucepan and simmer, covered, over a low heat for 10 minutes. Add 6 pieces each of the mangetout and broccoli and a pinch of the garlic and simmer, covered, for a further 10 minutes until completely soft. Transfer to a blender and add 3 tablespoons water. Pulse for 15 seconds, adding extra water 1 teaspoon at a time, until the mixture forms a lumpy purée. Serve warm.

chapter three
around the table

I find that I need a wide selection of dinners. There are weekdays when there isn't much time and I haven't planned ahead; weekends when I am happy to spend a little more time putting a meal together; and dinners with friends where I want to create something quite special. Whether you're feeling like meat, chicken or fish; beans or lentils; or anything from pasta to rice to more unusual grains, there are recipes to tempt you.

There are spring delights like Herb-Crusted Fish, summer favourites such as Open Quesadilla with Salsa, autumn treats like Pancetta-Wrapped Chicken with Quinoa Salad or winter stews such as Slowly Simmered Beef & Onion Stew. These will all provide you with wonderful meals for the whole family – whether they are 6-month olds or 60-year olds!

Pancetta-Wrapped Chicken with Quinoa Salad

SERVES: 2 adults, 1 child and 1 baby
PREPARATION TIME: 45 minutes, plus at least 7 hours soaking and 20 minutes cooking the quinoa
COOKING TIME: 40 minutes
STORAGE: Refrigerate the quinoa salad for up to 3 days. Refrigerate the chicken for up to 1 day.

1 tbsp extra virgin olive oil
1 tbsp finely chopped thyme leaves
½ tsp paprika
¼ tsp fine sea salt
6 boneless, skinless chicken thigh fillets
12 pancetta slices, sliced as thinly as possible, or 6 slices of Parma ham
freshly ground black pepper

FOR THE QUINOA SALAD
70g/2½oz/scant ½ cup frozen peas or fresh, podded peas
70g/2½oz green beans, trimmed and chopped
70g/2½oz broccoli, cut into bite-sized florets
1 small leek, quartered lengthways and sliced
1 recipe quantity cooked quinoa (see page 22)
1 tsp fine sea salt

FOR THE DRESSING
2 tbsp toasted sesame oil
2 tbsp extra virgin olive oil
1 tbsp red miso
4 tbsp brown rice vinegar

1 (6-9) (9-12) Preheat the oven to 200°C/400°F/gas 6 and grease the bottom of a baking dish with the oil. Mix the thyme, paprika and salt in a small, shallow bowl. Put the chicken thighs in the baking dish, then sprinkle the thyme mixture over the top and season with pepper. Wrap 2 slices of the pancetta (or 1 slice of Parma ham) around each thigh, tucking the ends underneath the thigh to secure them. Bake for 35–40 minutes until the chicken is cooked through and the pancetta has browned.

2 Meanwhile, make the quinoa salad. Put the vegetables in a steamer and steam, covered, for 3 minutes until tender. Put the steamed vegetables, cooked quinoa and salt in a large bowl and mix well.

3 To make the dressing, put all of the ingredients in a small jar. Secure with a lid and shake vigorously until the miso has completely dissolved. Pour the dressing over the salad and mix well. Serve warm with the chicken.

(6-9) **CHICKEN & QUINOA PURÉE WITH MIXED VEG PURÉE**
Put ½ of 1 chicken thigh, 2 tablespoons of the cooked quinoa and 135ml/4½fl oz/generous ½ cup boiling water in a greased baking dish. Bake as above for 20 minutes until the chicken is completely cooked through and the quinoa is completely soft. Transfer to a blender and add 4 tablespoons water. Blend for 30 seconds, adding extra water 1 teaspoon at a time, until smooth. Leave 3 broccoli pieces, 4 green bean pieces and 1 tablespoon of the peas in the steamer and steam, covered, for a further 7 minutes, until completely soft. Transfer to a blender and add 2 tablespoons water. Blend for 30 seconds, adding extra water 1 teaspoon at a time, until smooth. Serve warm with the chicken and quinoa purée.

 CHICKEN & QUINOA WITH MIXED VEG & LEEKS
Put ½ of 1 chicken thigh, 2 tablespoons of the cooked quinoa and 135ml/4½fl oz/generous ½ cup boiling water in a greased baking dish. Bake as above for 20 minutes until the chicken is completely cooked through and the quinoa is completely soft. Transfer to a blender and add 4 tablespoons water. Pulse for 15 seconds, adding extra water 1 teaspoon at a time, until the mixture forms a lumpy purée. Leave 3 broccoli pieces, 4 green bean pieces and 1 tablespoon each of the peas and leeks in the steamer and steam, covered, for a further 7 minutes until completely soft. Transfer to a blender and add 2 tablespoons water. Pulse for 15 seconds, adding extra water 1 teaspoon at a time, until the mixture forms a lumpy purée. Serve warm with the chicken and quinoa purée.

Chicken Piccata with Baked Sweet Potato & Apple

SERVES: 2 adults, 1 child and 1 baby
PREPARATION TIME: 40 minutes
COOKING TIME: 30 minutes
STORAGE: Refrigerate for up to 1 day.

....

2 sweet potatoes, cut into chunks
4 apples, cored and cut into chunks
2 tbsp wholemeal spelt flour or
    wholemeal plain flour
1 tsp fine sea salt
3 boneless, skinless chicken breast
    fillets, or 6 boneless, skinless chicken
    thigh fillets, each sliced horizontally
    into 2 flat pieces
30g/1oz unsalted butter
2 tbsp extra virgin olive oil, plus extra
    for greasing
6 tbsp lemon juice
1 small lemon, thinly sliced
240ml/8fl oz/scant 1 cup white
    wine
3 tbsp capers in salt or brine,
    drained and rinsed
6 tbsp chopped parsley leaves
freshly ground black pepper
steamed vegetables, to serve

1 Preheat the oven to 220°C/425°F/gas 7 and grease a large, shallow baking dish with oil. (6-9) (9-12) Put the sweet potatoes, apples and 80ml/ 2½fl oz/⅓ cup water in the baking dish and bake for 30 minutes until soft and lightly browned.

2 Meanwhile, mix the flour and salt in a shallow bowl and season with pepper. Dip each chicken piece into the flour to coat well, shake off any excess flour and transfer to a plate. Heat ½ of the butter and oil in a large, heavy-based frying pan over a medium-high heat. Working in batches to avoid overcrowding the pan, add the chicken and cook for 2–3 minutes on each side until the chicken is golden brown and cooked through. Remove from the pan and repeat with the remaining chicken, adding the remaining butter and oil to the pan as needed. Leave the cooked chicken to one side. Remove the pan from the heat and leave to cool slightly.

3 Add the lemon juice, lemon slices, wine, capers and parsley to the pan, then bring to the boil over a high heat. Turn the heat down to low and simmer, covered, for 10 minutes. Return the chicken to the pan and cook for 2–3 minutes until warmed through. Serve warm with the sauce poured over and with the baked sweet potatoes, apples and steamed vegetables.

(6-9) BAKED CHICKEN, SWEET POTATO & APPLE PURÉE
Put 50g/1¾oz of the chicken, 4 sweet potato chunks, 4 apple chunks and 2 tablespoons water in a baking dish and bake as above for 20 minutes until the chicken is completely cooked through and the juices run clear, and the sweet potato and apple are completely soft. Transfer to a blender and add 3 tablespoons water. Blend for 30 seconds, adding extra water 1 teaspoon at a time, until smooth. Serve warm.

(9-12) BAKED HERBY CHICKEN, SWEET POTATO & APPLE
Put 50g/1¾oz of the chicken, 2 sweet potato chunks, 4 apple chunks and 2 tablespoons water in a baking dish and bake as above for 20 minutes until the chicken is completely cooked through and the juices run clear, and the sweet potato and apple are completely soft. Transfer to a blender and add 1 teaspoon of the parsley and 3 tablespoons water. Pulse for 15 seconds, adding extra water 1 teaspoon at a time, until the mixture forms a lumpy purée. Serve warm.

This is my dad's favourite chicken dish – without the broccoli! He adores how the spicy ingredients are contrasted by a hint of sweetness. The totally gorgeous baby is Niamh Harrison-Murray, the daughter of my friends Nathalie and Diarmid. She is pictured here having some of her first purées.

Edward's Ginger Chicken

SERVES: 2 adults, 1 child and 1 baby
PREPARATION TIME: 30 minutes, plus at least 7 hours soaking and 35 minutes cooking the brown basmati rice
COOKING TIME: 50 minutes
STORAGE: Refrigerate the chicken and sauce for up to 1 day. Refrigerate the basmati rice for up to 3 days.

....

125ml/4fl oz/½ cup extra virgin olive oil
3 boneless, skinless chicken breast
    fillets or 6 boneless, skinless
    chicken thigh fillets
7 spring onions, finely sliced
2½ tbsp finely chopped root ginger
1½ tsp chilli powder
500ml/17fl oz/2 cups chicken stock
1 tsp black peppercorns
1 tbsp cane sugar
1 tbsp tamari soy sauce or shoyu
    soy sauce
1 tbsp cornflour, ground arrowroot
    or crushed kuzu
1 recipe quantity cooked brown
    basmati rice (see page 23)
1 tsp salt
steamed broccoli, cut into
    bite-sized florets, to serve

1 Heat the oil in a large, heavy-based frying pan over a medium-high heat. Add the chicken and cook for 3–4 minutes on each side until browned.

2 (6-9) (9-12) Add the spring onions, ginger, chilli powder, stock, peppercorns, sugar and tamari to the pan. Bring to the boil over a medium-high heat, then turn the heat down to low and simmer, covered, for 30–35 minutes until the chicken is tender and cooked through.

3 In a small bowl, mix the cornflour and 1 tablespoon cold water together to make a smooth paste. Remove the chicken from the frying pan and stir the cornflour mixture into the liquid remaining in the pan. Stir over a medium heat for 5 minutes or until the sauce is thick and glossy. Put the cooked brown basmati rice in a large bowl, add the salt and mix well. Serve the chicken with the sauce poured over the top and with the rice and steamed broccoli.

(6-9) CHICKEN, BROCCOLI & BROWN BASMATI RICE PURÉE
Put 2 tablespoons of the cooked brown basmati rice, 50g/1¾oz of the browned chicken and 135ml/4½fl oz/generous ½ cup boiling water in a saucepan. Bring to the boil over a high heat, then turn the heat down to low and simmer, covered, for 10 minutes. Add 2 tablespoons of steamed broccoli and simmer, covered, for a further 10 minutes until the rice is completely soft and the chicken is completely cooked through. Transfer to a blender and add 3 tablespoons water. Blend for 30 seconds, adding extra water 1 teaspoon at a time, until smooth. Serve warm.

(9-12) CHICKEN, VEGGIES & BROWN BASMATI RICE
Put 2 tablespoons of the cooked brown basmati rice, 50g/1¾oz of the browned chicken, 1 teaspoon of the spring onions and 135ml/4½fl oz/ generous ½ cup boiling water in a saucepan. Bring to the boil over a high heat, then turn the heat down to low and simmer, covered, for 10 minutes. Add 2 tablespoons of steamed broccoli and simmer, covered, for a further 10 minutes until the rice is completely soft and the chicken is completely cooked through. Transfer to a blender and add 3 tablespoons water. Pulse for 15 seconds, adding extra water 1 teaspoon at a time, until the mixture forms a lumpy purée. Serve warm.

Packed with toasted garlic, this simple and tasty chicken is gorgeous served with celeriac slaw. My friend Julia, in Tuscany, served it to her husband Dayton and a builder who was working at their house – and both men gave it the thumbs up.

Garlic Chicken with Celeriac Slaw

SERVES: 2 adults, 1 child and 1 baby
PREPARATION TIME: 30 minutes
COOKING TIME: 40 minutes
STORAGE: Refrigerate the chicken for up to 1 day. Refrigerate the slaw for up to 3 days.

....

30g/1oz unsalted butter, plus extra for greasing and serving
8 garlic cloves, sliced
3 boneless chicken breast fillets or 6 boneless chicken thigh fillets
1½ tsp balsamic vinegar
cooked corn spaghetti or gluten-free spaghetti, to serve
¼ tsp fine sea salt, to serve
2 tbsp extra virgin olive oil, to serve

FOR THE CELERIAC SLAW
1 celeriac, peeled and grated
1½ tbsp lemon juice
3 tbsp mayonnaise
1 tsp Dijon mustard
1 tsp poppy seeds
3 tbsp extra virgin olive oil

1 Preheat the oven to 200°C/400°F/gas 6 and grease a large baking dish with butter. Heat ½ of the butter in a heavy-based frying pan over a medium heat. Add the garlic and cook for 5 minutes until golden brown, then remove the pan from the heat. **(6-9) (9-12)** Put the chicken in the baking dish skin-side up. Make 2 slits in the top of each breast, cutting halfway through the meat, and stuff ⅓ of the garlic into each slit. Evenly sprinkle the balsamic vinegar over the chicken breasts and bake for 30–35 minutes until the chicken skin has crisped and the juices run clear.

2 Meanwhile, make the celeriac slaw. Put all of the ingredients in a large bowl and mix well.

3 Serve the chicken hot with the celeriac slaw and the cooked corn spaghetti tossed with salt, oil and the remaining butter.

(6-9) CHICKEN & CELERIAC PURÉE
Put ½ of 1 chicken breast in a greased baking dish, remove the skin and bake as above for 15–20 minutes until completely cooked through and the juices run clear. Put 2 tablespoons of the celeriac in a steamer and steam, covered, for 10 minutes until completely soft. Transfer to a blender and add the cooked chicken and 3 tablespoons water. Blend for 30 seconds, adding extra water 1 teaspoon at at time, until smooth. Mix in 1 teaspoon of the oil and serve warm.

(9-12) CHICKEN, CORN SPAGHETTI & GRATED CELERIAC
Put ½ of 1 chicken breast in a greased baking dish, remove the skin and bake as above for 15–20 minutes until completely cooked through and the juices run clear. Transfer to a blender and add 2 tablespoons of the celeriac, 2 tablespoons of chopped, cooked corn spaghetti and 3 tablespoons water. Pulse for 15 seconds, adding extra water 1 teaspoon at a time, until the mixture forms a lumpy purée. Mix in 1 teaspoon of the oil and serve warm.

Stews are a wonderful way to achieve excellent flavours in a dish without a lot of fuss – just throw it together and cook it on the hob or in the oven while you do other things.

Pork & Orange Stew

SERVES: 2 adults, 1 child and 1 baby
PREPARATION TIME: 40 minutes
COOKING TIME: 1 hour 20 minutes
STORAGE: Refrigerate for up to 1 day.

....

3 tbsp extra virgin olive oil
450g/1lb boneless pork shoulder,
    cut into large chunks
2 carrots, cut into batons
1 onion, finely chopped
2 garlic cloves, finely chopped
1 tbsp cornflour, ground arrowroot
    or crushed kuzu
6 plum tomatoes, finely chopped
1 tbsp rice malt syrup or cane sugar
1 tbsp orange zest
240ml/8fl oz/scant 1 cup chicken stock
240ml/8fl oz/scant 1 cup dry white wine
1 tsp fine sea salt
cooked rice noodles, to serve

1 (6-9) (9-12) Heat 2 tablespoons of the oil in a large, heavy-based saucepan over a medium-high heat. Working in batches to avoid overcrowding the pan, add the pork and cook, stirring frequently, for 6 minutes until well browned on all sides. Remove from the pan, using a slotted spoon, and set aside. Repeat with the remaining pork, adding the remaining oil to the pan as needed.

2 Return the pork to the pan and add the carrots, onion and garlic and cook for another 8 minutes until the vegetables are beginning to brown. In a small bowl, mix the cornflour and 1 tablespoon cold water together to make a smooth paste. Add the tomatoes, rice malt syrup, orange zest, stock, wine, cornflour mixture and salt and stir well. Bring to the boil over a medium-high heat, then turn the heat down to low and simmer, covered, for 1 hour until the pork is tender. Serve hot over cooked rice noodles.

(6-9) **PORK, RICE NOODLE & CARROT PURÉE**
Heat a heavy-based frying pan over a medium-low heat until hot.
Add 50g/1¾oz of the pork, 6 carrot pieces, 1 teaspoon of the oil and 6 tablespoons water. Simmer, covered, for 20 minutes until the pork is tender and completely cooked through and the carrots are completely soft. Transfer to a blender and add 2 tablespoons of chopped, cooked rice noodles. Blend for 30 seconds, adding water 1 teaspoon at a time, until smooth. Serve warm.

 PORK WITH RICE NOODLES & VEGETABLES
Heat a heavy-based frying pan over a medium-low heat until hot. Add 50g/1¾oz of the pork, 6 carrot pieces, 1 teaspoon of the onion, a pinch of the chopped garlic, 1 teaspoon of the oil and 6 tablespoons water. Simmer, covered, for 20 minutes until the pork is tender and completely cooked through and the carrots are completely soft. Transfer to a blender and add 2 tablespoons of chopped, cooked rice noodles. Pulse for 15 seconds, adding water 1 teaspoon at a time, until the mixture forms a lumpy purée. Serve warm.

Pork with Capers & Celeriac Mash

SERVES: 2 adults, 1 child and 1 baby
PREPARATION TIME: 30 minutes
COOKING TIME: 1 hour 35 minutes
STORAGE: Refrigerate the pork for
up to 1 day. Refrigerate the mash
for up to 3 days.

....

30g/1oz unsalted butter
3 large pork chops or 6 regular
    pork chops
2 onions, finely chopped
3 garlic cloves, finely chopped
1 tbsp tomato purée
25g/1oz drained, bottled or tinned
    anchovies in oil, chopped
455ml/16fl oz/scant 2 cups chicken
    stock
2 tbsp capers in salt or brine,
    drained and rinsed
1½ tbsp chopped parsley leaves
freshly ground black pepper
steamed vegetables, to serve

FOR THE CELERIAC MASH
1 celeriac, peeled and cut into chunks
500g/1lb 2oz potatoes, peeled and
    cut into chunks
50g/1¾oz unsalted butter
4 tbsp extra virgin olive oil
1 tbsp coarse grain mustard
120ml/4fl oz/½ cup vegetable stock
freshly ground black pepper

1 Heat ½ of the butter in a large, heavy-based frying pan over a medium-high heat until melted. (6-9) (9-12) Working in batches, add the pork chops and fry for 3–5 minutes on each side until browned. Transfer to a plate and season with pepper. Repeat with the remaining pork chops, adding the remaining butter to the pan as needed.

2 Reduce the heat to medium. Add the onions to the pan and fry for 5 minutes until beginning to brown. Add the garlic, tomato purée, anchovies and stock and mix. Bring to the boil over a high heat, stirring with a wooden spoon to lift the dark coating off the bottom of the pan. Return the pork to the pan, turn the heat down to low and simmer, covered, for 30 minutes. Turn the chops over and simmer, covered, for a further 30 minutes. Add the capers and cook for 10 minutes until the pork is tender.

3 Meanwhile, make the celeriac mash. Put the celeriac and potatoes into separate pans of cold water and bring to the boil over a high heat. Reduce the heat to medium and simmer, covered, cooking the celeriac for 15–20 minutes and the potatoes for 10–12 minutes or until both are tender. Drain well and transfer the celeriac and potatoes into one pan. Mash the celeriac and potatoes together thoroughly, then mix in the butter, oil and mustard until well combined. Stir in enough stock to make the mash creamy and smooth, then season with pepper to taste. Sprinkle the pork with parsley and serve hot over the celeriac mash with steamed vegetables.

(6-9) PORK & CELERIAC PURÉE
Cut 50g/1¾oz of the pork into small pieces. Put the pork, 4 tablespoons of the cooked celeriac (without the other ingredients) and 240ml/8fl oz/scant 1 cup boiling water in a saucepan. Simmer, covered, over a low heat for 20 minutes until the pork is completely cooked through. Transfer to a blender and blend for 30 seconds, adding water 1 teaspoon at a time, until smooth. Serve warm.

 PORK, ANCHOVY & CELERIAC
Cut 50g/1¾oz of the pork into small pieces. Put the pork, 4 tablespoons of the cooked celeriac (without the other ingredients), 1 anchovy piece and 240ml/8fl oz/scant 1 cup boiling water in a saucepan. Simmer, covered, over a low heat for 20 minutes until the pork is completely cooked through. Transfer to a blender and pulse for 15 seconds, adding water 1 teaspoon at a time, until the mixture forms a lumpy purée. Serve warm.

Lamb Biryani

SERVES: 2 adults, 1 child and 1 baby
PREPARATION TIME: 30 minutes, plus
at least 7 hours soaking, plus at least
2 hours marinating
COOKING TIME: 1 hour 10 minutes
STORAGE: Refrigerate for up to 1 day.

....

300g/10½oz/1½ cups brown basmati
    or long grain rice
1½ tbsp natural yogurt or kefir, for
    soaking
500g/1lb 2oz boneless leg of lamb,
    trimmed of fat and cut into chunks
¼ tsp saffron threads
3 tbsp extra virgin olive oil or ghee
3 onions, halved and thinly sliced
1½ tsp fine sea salt
steamed mangetout, to serve

FOR THE MARINADE
185ml/6fl oz/¾ cup natural yogurt
1 tbsp lemon juice or white wine
    vinegar
2 fresh green chillies, halved,
    deseeded and thinly sliced
1 tbsp grated root ginger
3 garlic cloves, crushed
1½ tsp ground coriander
1 tsp paprika
¼ tsp turmeric
½ tsp ground cumin
½ tsp chilli powder
¼ tsp ground cinnamon
¼ tsp ground cardamom
¼ tsp ground cloves
1 tsp fine sea salt

1 (6-9) (9-18) Put the rice, yogurt and 800ml/28fl oz/scant 3½ cups water in a large saucepan and leave to soak, covered, for 7 hours or overnight at room temperature.

2 To make the marinade, put all of the ingredients in a non-reactive bowl and mix well. Add the lamb and stir well, making sure the lamb is covered in the marinade. Cover and leave to marinate in the fridge for 2 hours or overnight.

3 Put the saffron in a small bowl, cover with 1 tablespoon warm water and leave to soak. Heat the oil in a large, heavy-based saucepan or casserole dish over a medium heat. Add the onions and fry for 5 minutes until beginning to brown, then turn the heat up to medium-high. Add the rice and soaking water, salt and the saffron mixture and bring to the boil over a high heat, then turn the heat down to low.

4 Add the lamb and the marinade and simmer, covered, for 1 hour until the lamb is tender and the rice is soft. Gently stir the lamb and rice together until they are mixed well. Serve hot with steamed mangetout.

(6-9) LAMB, MANGETOUT & BROWN RICE PURÉE
Put 4 tablespoons of the brown rice, 1 teaspoon of the yogurt and 240ml/8fl oz/scant 1 cup water in a heavy-based saucepan and leave to soak, covered, for 7 hours or overnight at room temperature. Add 50g/1¾oz of the lamb and bring to the boil over a medium-high heat. Turn the heat down to low and simmer, covered, for 50 minutes. Add 4 steamed mangetout and simmer, covered, for a further 10 minutes until the lamb is completely cooked through and the rice is completely soft. Transfer to a blender and blend for 30 seconds, adding water 1 teaspoon at a time, until smooth. Mix in 1 teaspoon of the oil and serve warm.

(9-12) LAMB STEW
Put 4 tablespoons of the brown rice, 1 teaspoon of the yogurt and 240ml/8fl oz/scant 1 cup water in a heavy-based saucepan and leave to soak, covered, for 7 hours or overnight at room temperature. Add 50g/1¾oz of the lamb, 1 teaspoon of the onion and a pinch of the garlic and bring to the boil over a medium-high heat. Turn the heat down to low and simmer, covered, for 50 minutes. Add 4 steamed mangetout and simmer, covered, for a further 10 minutes until the lamb is completely cooked through and the rice is completely soft. Transfer to a blender and pulse for 15 seconds, adding water 1 teaspoon at a time, until the mixture forms a lumpy purée. Mix in 1 teaspoon of the oil and serve warm.

The lamb in this tagine is cooked slowly with a mix of spices, sweet orange juice, apricots and ginger. Leave it in the oven until all the flavours have married together and everything is tender – and really, really delicious.

Lamb Tagine

SERVES: 2 adults, 1 child and 1 baby
PREPARATION TIME: 45 minutes, plus at least 7 hours soaking and 20 minutes cooking the quinoa
COOKING TIME: 2½–3 hours
STORAGE: Refrigerate for up to 1 day.

....

2 tbsp extra virgin olive oil, plus extra for frying if needed
450g/1lb boneless lamb shoulder, trimmed of fat and cut into chunks
1 small onion, finely chopped
80ml/2½fl oz/⅓ cup freshly squeezed orange juice
200g/7oz squash, deseeded and cut into bite-sized pieces or pumpkin, peeled, deseeded and cut into bite-sized pieces
12–15 cherry tomatoes, halved
110g/3¾oz/scant ⅔ cup dried unsulphured apricots, finely chopped
2 tsp grated root ginger
1 garlic clove, finely chopped
1 tsp ground cinnamon
¾ tsp ground coriander
¼ tsp ground cloves
½ tsp paprika
½ tsp turmeric
½ tsp ground cumin
1 tbsp wholemeal spelt flour or wholemeal plain flour
1 tsp fine sea salt
1 recipe quantity cooked quinoa (see page 22), to serve

1 Preheat the oven to 150°C/300°F/gas 2. Heat the oil in a large, flameproof casserole dish over a medium-high heat. **(6-9)** **(9-12)** Working in batches to avoid overcrowding the pan, add the lamb and fry, stirring frequently, for 5 minutes until well browned on all sides. Remove from the pan, using a slotted spoon, and set aside. Repeat with the remaining lamb, adding more oil to the pan as needed.

2 Return the lamb to the pan. Add all of the remaining ingredients and 240ml/8fl oz/scant 1 cup boiling water and mix well.

3 Transfer to the oven and bake, covered, for 2–2½ hours until the lamb is completely tender. Serve hot over the cooked quinoa.

(6-9) LAMB, SQUASH, APRICOT & QUINOA PURÉE
Put 50g/1¾oz of the lamb, 6 squash pieces, 1 teaspoon of the apricots and 240ml/8fl oz/scant 1 cup water in a casserole dish. Bake as above, covered, for 20 minutes. Add 2 tablespoons of the cooked quinoa and bake, covered, for a further 20 minutes until completely soft and the lamb is completely cooked through. Transfer to a blender and blend for 30 seconds, adding water 1 teaspoon at a time, until smooth. Serve warm.

(9-12) LAMB & QUINOA STEW
Put 50g/1¾oz of the lamb, 6 squash pieces, 1 teaspoon of the apricots, ½ teaspoon of the onion and 240ml/8fl oz/scant 1 cup water in a casserole dish. Bake as above, covered, for 20 minutes. Add 2 tablespoons of the cooked quinoa and bake, covered, for a further 20 minutes until completely soft and the lamb is completely cooked through. Transfer to a blender and pulse for 15 seconds, adding water 1 teaspoon at a time, until the mixture forms a lumpy purée. Serve warm.

Slowly Simmered Beef & Onion Stew

SERVES: 2 adults, 1 child and 1 baby
PREPARATION TIME: 30 minutes
COOKING TIME: 2½ hours
STORAGE: Refrigerate for up to
1 day, or freeze for up to 1 month.

. . . .

½ tbsp wholemeal spelt flour or
    wholemeal plain flour
1 tsp fine sea salt
¼ tsp freshly ground black pepper
450g/1lb braising steak, trimmed
    of fat and cut into chunks
1½ tbsp extra virgin olive oil
2 large onions, halved and thinly sliced
1 garlic clove, finely chopped
½ tsp finely chopped thyme leaves
1 bay leaf
1 tsp finely chopped root ginger
90ml/3fl oz/⅓ cup dark beer
1½ tbsp cider vinegar or grape vinegar
1½ tbsp chopped parsley leaves
steamed sweet potatoes, thickly sliced,
    to serve
steamed cauliflower, to serve

1 In a large bowl, mix together the flour, ½ teaspoon of the salt and the pepper. (6-9) (9-12) Add the beef and toss well, making sure the beef is coated in the flour mixture. Heat ½ tablespoon of the oil in a large, heavy-based saucepan over a medium-high heat. Working in batches to avoid overcrowding the pan, add the beef and cook for 3–4 minutes on each side until well browned. Remove the beef from the pan, using a slotted spoon, transfer to a large bowl and set aside. Repeat with the remaining beef, adding another 1 teaspoon of oil to the pan before cooking each batch.

2 Reduce the heat to medium and add ½ tablespoon of the oil, the onions and the remaining salt. Cook, stirring occasionally, for 5 minutes until the onions are beginning to brown. Add the garlic, thyme, bay leaf, ginger and 30ml/1fl oz/2 tablespoons water. Using a wooden spoon, lift the dark coating off the bottom of the pan. Cook for 2 minutes, until all the brown coating has dissolved. Slowly add the beer and cider vinegar, then return the beef and any juices from the bowl to the pan.

3 Bring to the boil over a medium-high heat, then turn the heat down to low and simmer, covered, for 2 hours, stirring occasionally, until the beef is tender and cooked through. Remove the bay leaf and stir in the parsley. Serve hot with steamed sweet potatoes and cauliflower.

(6-9)

FRIED BEEF & CAULIFLOWER PURÉE WITH SWEET POTATO MASH

Heat a heavy-based frying pan over a medium heat until hot. Add 50g/1¾oz of the beef and 3 steamed cauliflower florets and dry-fry, covered, for 10 minutes until lightly browned and completely cooked through. Transfer to a blender and add 3 tablespoons water. Blend for 30 seconds, adding extra water 1 teaspoon at a time, until smooth. Serve warm with mashed, steamed sweet potato.

(9-12)

FRIED BEEF & VEGETABLES WITH SWEET POTATO MASH

Heat a heavy-based frying pan over a medium heat. Add 50g/1¾oz of the beef, ½ a slice of onion, 3 steamed cauliflower florets and a pinch of the garlic. Dry-fry, covered, for 10 minutes until lightly browned and completely cooked through. Transfer to a blender and add 3 tablespoons water. Pulse for 15 seconds, adding extra water 1 teaspoon at a time, until the mixture forms a lumpy purée. Serve warm with mashed, steamed sweet potato.

Louisiana Beef Grillade

SERVES: 2 adults, 1 child and 1 baby
PREPARATION TIME: 40 minutes
COOKING TIME: 1 hour 10 minutes
STORAGE: Refrigerate for up to 1 day.

....

4 tbsp wholemeal spelt flour or
   wholemeal plain flour
1½ tsp fine sea salt
4 fillet steaks, sliced into strips
3 tbsp extra virgin olive oil
1 onion, quartered and thinly sliced
2 celery stalks, halved lengthways
   and chopped
1 orange pepper, halved, deseeded
   and diced
2 garlic cloves, finely chopped
240ml/8fl oz/scant 1 cup beef stock
300g/10½oz tinned chopped tomatoes
½ tbsp finely chopped thyme leaves
   or ½ tsp dried thyme
½ tbsp chopped basil leaves
   or ½ tsp dried basil
½ tsp crushed chillies
4 tbsp chopped parsley leaves
150g/5½oz/1 cup grits or polenta
115g/4oz unsalted butter
freshly ground black pepper
steamed, shelled broad beans,
   to serve

1 Put 2 tablespoons of the flour and ½ teaspoon of the salt in a large, shallow bowl. (6-9) (9-12) Season with pepper and mix, then add the beef and toss well, making sure the beef is coated in the flour mixture.

2 Heat 2 tablespoons of the oil in a large, heavy-based frying pan over a medium-high heat. Add the beef and cook, stirring frequently, for 6 minutes until browned. Remove the beef from the pan, using a slotted spoon, and set aside.

3 Add the remaining oil to the pan, followed by the onion, celery and pepper. Cook, stirring occasionally, for 5 minutes until tender. Stir in the garlic and the remaining flour and cook for another 5 minutes. Add the stock and 240ml/8fl oz/scant 1 cup water and mix.

4 Return the beef to the pan and add the tinned tomatoes, thyme, basil, crushed chillies and parsley. Turn the heat down to low and simmer, covered, for 45–50 minutes until the beef is completely tender.

5 Meanwhile, pour 950ml/32fl oz/scant 4 cups water into a large saucepan and bring to the boil over a high heat. Add the grits, whisking continuously with a whisk until smooth. Reduce the heat to medium-low and simmer, stirring continuously with a wooden spoon, for 20 minutes until the grits are thick and rubbery. Remove from the heat, add the butter and the remaining salt and mix well. Serve hot with the beef and steamed broad beans.

(6-9) BEEF & BROAD BEAN PURÉE
Heat a heavy-based frying pan over a medium-high heat until hot. Add 50g/1¾oz of the beef and 2 tablespoons of steamed broad beans and dry-fry for 10 minutes until the beef is completely cooked through. Transfer to a blender and add 4 tablespoons water. Blend for 30 seconds, adding extra water 1 teaspoon at a time, until smooth. Serve warm.

(9-12) BEEF, BROAD BEAN, ONION & GRITS
Heat a heavy-based frying pan over a medium-high heat until hot. Add 50g/1¾oz of the beef, 2 tablespoons of steamed broad beans, 1 teaspoon of the onion and a pinch of the parsley. Dry-fry for 10 minutes until the beef is completely cooked through. Transfer to a blender and add 4 tablespoons of the cooked grits (without the butter or salt) and 4 tablespoons water. Pulse for 15 seconds, adding extra water 1 teaspoon at a time, until the mixture forms a lumpy purée. Serve warm.

My sister Jan's husband is Egyptian and his mother taught her to make this delicious old-world family favourite. It's the Egyptian version of beef stew, which simmers slowly for a long time until the steak and celery almost melt away. With soul-warming potatoes, green beans and onion, it's the perfect fare for cold winter nights.

Egyptian Beef

SERVES: 2 adults, 1 child and 1 baby
PREPARATION TIME: 30 minutes, plus at least 7 hours soaking and 20 minutes cooking the buckwheat
COOKING TIME: 2–2½ hours
STORAGE: Refrigerate for up to 1 day.

....

450g/1lb sirloin joint, trimmed of fat and cut into chunks
½ tsp fine sea salt
¼ tsp freshly ground black pepper
1 onion, chopped
2 large celery stalks, halved lengthways and chopped
455ml/16fl oz/scant 2 cups chicken stock
1 large potato, quartered and sliced
225g/8oz green beans
3½ tbsp tomato purée
2 recipe quantities cooked buckwheat (see page 22)

1 Heat a large, heavy-based saucepan over a medium-high heat until hot. Add the beef and cook, stirring occasionally, for 6 minutes until browned. Add the salt and pepper and mix well.

2 Add the onion, celery and stock to the pan. Bring to the boil over a medium-high heat, then turn the heat down to low and simmer, covered, for 1½–2 hours until the celery and sirloin are meltingly tender.

3 Add the potato, green beans and tomato purée and cook for another 15 minutes or until the potatoes and beans are tender. Serve hot over the cooked buckwheat.

(6-9) BEEF, GREEN BEANS & BUCKWHEAT PURÉE
Cut 50g/1¾oz of the beef into small pieces, then cut 2 of the green beans into quarters. Put the beef and green beans in a saucepan, add 4 tablespoons of the cooked buckwheat and 135ml/4½fl oz/generous ½ cup water. Bring to the boil over a medium-high heat, then turn the heat down to low and simmer, covered, for 20 minutes until the beef is completely cooked through and the beans are completely soft. Transfer to a blender and add 3 tablespoons water. Blend for 30 seconds, adding extra water 1 teaspoon at a time, until smooth. Serve warm.

(9-12) BEEF, GREEN BEANS, ONION & BUCKWHEAT
Cut 50g/1¾oz of the beef into small pieces, then cut 2 of the green beans into quarters. Put the beef and green beans in a saucepan, add 4 tablespoons of the cooked buckwheat, 1 teaspoon of the onion and 135ml/4½fl oz/generous ½ cup water. Bring to the boil over a medium-high heat, then turn the heat down to low and simmer, covered, for 20 minutes until the beef is completely cooked through and the beans are completely soft. Transfer to a blender and add 3 tablespoons water. Pulse for 15 seconds, adding extra water 1 teaspoon at a time, until the mixture forms a lumpy purée. Serve warm.

Chinese Beef Stir-Fry

SERVES: 2 adults, 1 child and 1 baby
PREPARATION TIME: 35 minutes,
plus 1½ hours marinating, plus at
least 7 hours soaking and
40 minutes cooking the brown rice
COOKING TIME: 20 minutes
STORAGE: Refrigerate for up to 1 day.

....

3 sirloin steaks, cut into chunks
2 tbsp sesame oil
225g/8oz broccoli, cut into bite-sized
    florets
225g/8oz cauliflower, cut into
    bite-sized florets
1 recipe quantity cooked brown rice
    (see page 23), to serve

FOR THE MARINADE
3 tbsp tamari soy sauce or shoyu
    soy sauce
2 tbsp mirin
6 garlic cloves, finely chopped

FOR THE SAUCE
1 tbsp cornflour, ground arrowroot
    or crushed kuzu
125ml/4fl oz/½ cup vegetable stock
1½ tbsp mirin
1 tsp tamari soy sauce or shoyu
    soy sauce
1 tbsp toasted sesame oil
1½ tsp finely chopped root ginger

1 (9-12) To make the marinade, put all of the ingredients in a large, non-reactive bowl and mix well. (6-9) Add the beef and stir well, making sure the beef is covered in the marinade. Cover and leave to marinate in the fridge for 1½ hours.

2 To make the sauce, mix the cornflour and 1 tablespoon cold water together to make a smooth paste in a bowl. Add all of the remaining ingredients for the sauce and mix well.

3 Heat 1 tablespoon of the sesame oil in a wok or large frying pan over a medium-high heat. Using a slotted spoon, add the beef to the pan and reserve the marinade. Stir-fry over a medium-high heat for 6 minutes until browned. Remove the beef from the wok and set aside.

4 Reduce the heat to medium and add the remaining sesame oil. Add the marinade and bring to the boil. Cook for 1 minute, then add the broccoli and cauliflower and cook, stirring occasionally, for 5 minutes. Return the beef to the wok and add the sauce. Cook, stirring continuously, for another 3 minutes until the sauce has thickened, the beef is warmed through and the vegetables are just tender. Serve hot over the cooked brown rice.

(6-9) BEEF, CAULIFLOWER, BROCCOLI & RICE PURÉE
Put 4 tablespoons of the cooked brown rice in a saucepan, add 135ml/4½fl oz/generous ½ cup boiling water and simmer, covered, over a low heat for 20 minutes until completely soft. Heat 1 teaspoon of the sesame oil in a wok. Add 50g/1¾oz of the beef and 3 pieces each of the broccoli and cauliflower and cook for 15 minutes until the beef is completely cooked through and the vegetables are completely soft. Transfer to a blender and add the rice and 3 tablespoons water. Blend for 30 seconds, adding extra water 1 teaspoon at a time, until smooth. Serve warm.

 GARLIC BEEF, CAULIFLOWER, BROCCOLI & BROWN RICE
Put 4 tablespoons of the cooked brown rice in a saucepan, add 135ml/4½fl oz/generous ½ cup boiling water and simmer, covered, over a low heat for 20 minutes until completely soft. Heat 1 teaspoon of the sesame oil in a wok. Add 50g/1¾oz of the beef, ½ teaspoon of the garlic and 3 pieces each of the broccoli and cauliflower and cook for 15 minutes until the beef is completely cooked through and the vegetables are completely soft. Transfer to a blender and add the rice and 3 tablespoons water. Pulse for 15 seconds, adding extra water 1 teaspoon at a time, until the mixture forms a lumpy purée. Serve warm.

These flavours are simple, but great. When you serve this with sweet potatoes, you enjoy an excellent source of beta-carotene to raise blood levels of vitamin A, which is important for growth in children.

Herb-Crusted Fish

SERVES: 2 adults, 1 child and 1 baby
PREPARATION TIME: 15 minutes
COOKING TIME: 13 minutes
STORAGE: Refrigerate for up to 1 day.

....

150g/5½oz boneless salmon fillets
150g/5½oz boneless sea bream fillets
1 tbsp wholemeal spelt flour or wholemeal plain flour, for dusting
1½ tbsp extra virgin olive oil, plus extra for greasing
3 tbsp lime or lemon juice
2 tbsp dried wholemeal breadcrumbs
½ spring onion, finely chopped
1 garlic clove, finely chopped
1 tbsp chopped parsley leaves
1 tbsp finely chopped thyme leaves or 1 tsp dried thyme
¼ tsp fine sea salt
4 large, baked sweet potatoes, to serve
300g/10½oz steamed, shelled broad beans, to serve
lemon wedges, to serve

1 (6-9) (9-18) Preheat the oven to 200°C/400°F/gas 6 and grease a baking dish with oil. Coat the flesh (not the skin side) of the fish fillets in flour to make a dry surface for the herb mixture to stick to. Shake off any excess flour and transfer, skin-side down, to the baking dish.

2 Put the oil, lime juice, breadcrumbs, spring onion, garlic, parsley, thyme and salt in a small bowl and mix well. Spread the herb mixture evenly over the top of each fish.

3 Bake for about 10 minutes until the salmon is opaque and cooked through and the sea bream is white and flaky, then preheat the grill to medium-high. Put the fish under the grill for 3 minutes until the topping is golden brown. Serve hot with the baked sweet potatoes, steamed broad beans and lemon wedges.

(6-9) SALMON, BROAD BEAN & SWEET POTATO PURÉE
Remove the skin and rub oil over 50g/1¾oz of the salmon. Transfer to a baking dish and add 2 tablespoons of steamed broad beans and 2 tablespoons water. Bake as above for 10 minutes until the salmon is opaque and completely cooked through. Transfer to a blender and add 2 tablespoons of baked sweet potato flesh and 3 tablespoons water. Blend for 30 seconds, adding extra water 1 teaspoon at a time, until smooth. Serve warm.

(9-12) HERBY SALMON WITH BROAD BEANS & SWEET POTATO
Remove the skin and rub oil over 50g/1¾oz of the salmon. Transfer to a baking dish and add 2 tablespoons of steamed broad beans and 2 tablespoons water. Sprinkle with 1 teaspoon of the spring onion and a pinch each of the garlic and parsley and bake as above for 10 minutes until the salmon is opaque and completely cooked through. Transfer to a blender and add 2 tablespoons of baked sweet potato flesh and 3 tablespoons water. Pulse for 15 seconds, adding extra water 1 teaspoon at a time, until the mixture forms a lumpy purée. Serve warm.

Fragrant and succulent, this combines beautiful flavours from the fish, vegetables and spices. You can lift it out of the pot gently to keep the potatoes intact or break it up for a dense, chunky stew. It's a complete meal on its own, but it's good served with pitta bread to mop up the sauce.

Moroccan Fish

SERVES: 2 adults, 1 child and 1 baby
PREPARATION TIME: 35 minutes, plus at least 7 hours soaking and 40 minutes cooking the brown rice
COOKING TIME: 30 minutes
STORAGE: Refrigerate for up to 1 day.

....

4 tbsp extra virgin olive oil, plus extra to serve
2 onions, finely sliced
4 potatoes, finely sliced
4 carrots, sliced
6 plum tomatoes, sliced
8 garlic cloves, sliced
150g/5½oz boneless, skinless haddock or pollock fillets, cut into chunks
150g/5½oz boneless, skinless salmon fillets, cut into chunks
2 tbsp finely chopped coriander leaves
1 tsp ground cumin
1 tsp paprika
1½ tsp fine sea salt
1 recipe quantity cooked brown rice (see page 23), to serve

1 Put 2 tablespoons of the oil in a large, heavy-based frying pan with a tight-fitting lid. **(9-12)** Arrange the onions in a layer on the bottom of the pan. **(6-9)** Add 2 layers of the potatoes, followed by the carrots, tomatoes and garlic. Put the fish on top of the vegetables and pour in the remaining oil. Sprinkle the coriander, cumin, paprika and salt over the top of the fish.

2 Cook, covered, over a medium heat for 20–30 minutes until the haddock is white and flaky, the salmon is opaque and cooked through, the potatoes are soft and the juices from the fish and the vegetables have combined to form a sauce. Serve with the cooked brown rice.

(6-9) SALMON, CARROTS & BROWN RICE PURÉE
Put 4 tablespoons of the cooked brown rice, 2 tablespoons of the carrots and 135ml/4½fl oz/generous ½ cup boiling water in a saucepan and simmer, covered, for 10 minutes. Add 50g/1¾oz of the salmon and cook for a further 10 minutes until the salmon is opaque and completely cooked through and the carrots are completely soft. Transfer to a blender and add 4 tablespoons water. Blend for 30 seconds, adding extra water 1 teaspoon at a time, until smooth. Mix in 1 teaspoon of the oil and serve warm.

(9-12) SALMON WITH VEGGIES & BROWN RICE
Put 4 tablespoons of the cooked brown rice, 2 tablespoons of the carrots and 135ml/4½fl oz/generous ½ cup boiling water in a saucepan and simmer, covered, for 10 minutes. Add 50g/1¾oz of the salmon and 1 teaspoon of the onion and cook for a further 10 minutes until the salmon is opaque and completely cooked through and the vegetables are completely soft. Transfer to a blender and add 4 tablespoons water. Pulse for 15 seconds, adding extra water 1 teaspoon at a time, until the mixture forms a lumpy purée. Mix in 1 teaspoon of the oil and serve warm.

Fish Pie

SERVES: 2 adults, 1 child and 1 baby
PREPARATION TIME: 40 minutes,
plus 30 minutes chilling
COOKING TIME: 1 hour
STORAGE: Refrigerate for up to 1 day.

....

unsalted butter, for greasing
1 large sweet potato, diced
1 large potato, diced
1 carrot, halved lengthways and sliced
200g/7oz boneless, skinless pollock
   or hake fillets, cut into chunks
200g/7oz boneless, skinless salmon
   fillets, cut into chunks
5 shallots, chopped
salad, to serve

FOR THE PASTRY
120g/4¼oz/1 cup wholemeal spelt flour
   or wholemeal plain flour, plus extra
   for dusting
¼ tsp fine sea salt
60g/2¼oz chilled, unsalted butter, diced

FOR THE SAUCE
3 tbsp extra virgin olive oil
3 tbsp wholemeal spelt flour or
   wholemeal plain flour
250ml/9fl oz/1 cup vegetable stock
2 tsp chopped rosemary leaves
½ tsp fine sea salt

1 To make the pastry, mix the flour and salt in a large bowl and rub in the butter with your fingertips until the mixture resembles breadcrumbs. Sprinkle 3–4 tablespoons cold water into the mixture, 1 tablespoon at a time, and mix with a fork until the dough is beginning to hold together. Shape the pastry into a ball, wrap in cling film and chill in the fridge for 30 minutes.

2 Preheat the oven to 200°C/400°F/gas 6 and grease a 25cm/10in pie dish with butter. (6-9) (9-12) Meanwhile, put the potatoes and carrot in a steamer and steam, covered, for 10 minutes until just tender. Put the potatoes, carrot, fish and shallots in a large bowl and mix well.

3 To make the sauce, mix the oil and flour in a heavy-based saucepan and cook, stirring continuously, over a medium heat for 1 minute. Remove the pan from the heat and gradually add the stock, rosemary and salt. Return the pan to a medium-low heat and cook, stirring continuously, for 5 minutes until thickened and smooth.

4 Add the sauce to the fish mixture and mix well. Pour the mixture into the pie dish and smooth the top with the back of a wooden spoon. Dust a piece of baking parchment with flour. Roll out the pastry into a circle about 25cm/10in in diameter and trim around the edges, using a sharp knife, to neaten. Ease the pastry onto the top of the pie dish and cover the filling, then press down around the rim of the pie dish with your fingers to seal and crimp the edge. Using a sharp knife, cut a small cross in the centre of the pastry lid. Bake for 40 minutes until the pastry is golden brown. Serve warm with salad.

 SALMON, SWEET POTATO & CARROT PURÉE
Finely chop 2 tablespoons each of the carrot and sweet potato. Transfer to a ramekin and add 50g/1¾oz of the salmon and 2 tablespoons water. Bake as above for 15 minutes until the salmon is opaque and completely cooked through. Transfer to a blender and add 3 tablespoons water. Blend for 30 seconds, adding extra water 1 teaspoon at a time, until smooth. Serve warm.

(9-12) **POLLOCK WITH SWEET POTATO, SHALLOTS & CARROTS**
Finely chop 1 tablespoon of the carrot and 2 tablespoons of the sweet potato. Transfer to a ramekin and add 50g/1¾oz of the pollock, 2 shallot pieces and 2 tablespoons water. Bake as above for 15 minutes until the pollock is completely cooked through. Transfer to a blender and add 3 tablespoons water. Pulse for 15 seconds, adding extra water 1 teaspoon at a time, until the mixture forms a lumpy purée. Serve warm.

Packed with flavour and fresh, bright vegetables, here's a meal that's beautiful to see and to eat. Whenever I make this dish, my friends always ask for the recipe – it's a true crowd-pleaser.

Noodles with Saucy Squid

SERVES: 2 adults, 1 child and 1 baby
PREPARATION TIME: 35 minutes
COOKING TIME: 10 minutes
STORAGE: Refrigerate for up to 1 day.

....

2 tbsp extra virgin olive oil
1 carrot, cut into matchsticks
1 small yellow pepper, halved, deseeded and cut into matchsticks
1 small red pepper, deseeded and cut into matchsticks
1 courgette, cut into matchsticks
70g/2½oz/scant ½ cup defrosted, frozen peas or fresh, podded peas
4 tbsp lemon juice
80ml/2½fl oz/⅓ cup dry white wine
300g/10½oz squid tubes, cut into rings
300g/10½oz 100% buckwheat soba noodles or brown rice noodles

FOR THE SAUCE
3 garlic cloves, chopped
2 tbsp extra virgin olive oil
4 tbsp chopped basil leaves, 4 tbsp grated Parmesan cheese and ¼ tsp fine sea salt or 8 tbsp unsweetened, desiccated coconut and 1 tsp fine sea salt

1 (6-9) (9-12) To make the sauce, mix all of the ingredients in a small bowl, then cover and set aside.

2 Heat the oil in a wok or large frying pan over a medium-high heat. Add the carrot and stir-fry for 3 minutes, then add the peppers and courgette and stir-fry for another 2 minutes. Add the peas and stir-fry for 1 minute until the carrot and peppers are tender but remain quite crunchy. Remove the vegetables from the pan and transfer to a large bowl. Sprinkle with the lemon juice and mix well.

3 Add the wine to the wok and bring to the boil over a high heat. Reduce the heat to medium and add the squid. Simmer for 3 minutes until the squid is just cooked and tender. Add the sauce and mix well.

4 Meanwhile, cook the noodles in plenty of boiling water, according to the packet instructions, and drain well. Serve warm topped with the saucy squid and vegetables.

(6-9) CARROT, COURGETTE, COCONUT, PEA & NOODLE PURÉE
Put 1½ tablespoons each of the carrot, courgette and peas in a steamer and steam, covered, for 10 minutes until completely soft. Transfer to a blender and add 2 tablespoons of chopped, cooked noodles (without the saucy squid), 1 tablespoon of the coconut and 3 tablespoons water. Blend for 30 seconds, adding extra water 1 teaspoon at a time, until smooth. Mix in 1 teaspoon of the oil and serve warm.

 NOODLES WITH VEG & COCONUT
Put 1 tablespoon each of the carrot, courgette and peas in a steamer and steam, covered, for 10 minutes until completely soft. Transfer to a blender and add 2 tablespoons of chopped, cooked noodles (without the saucy squid), 1 tablespoon of the coconut and 3 tablespoons water. Pulse for 15 seconds, adding extra water 1 teaspoon at a time, until the mixture forms a lumpy purée. Mix in 1 teaspoon of the oil and serve warm.

My brother David has perfected this dish over the years and is sweet enough to make it for me when we are home for the holidays. He serves it as a starter, but I also love it over rice as a main meal. Spiced with jalapeño and chilli, it also has lime and cumin, which are heavenly.

Spicy Avocado Prawns

SERVES: 2 adults, 1 child and 1 baby
PREPARATION TIME: 20 minutes
COOKING TIME: 10 minutes
STORAGE: Use the same day.

....

300g/10½oz brown rice noodles
1 tsp fine sea salt
6 tbsp extra virgin olive oil
225g/8oz raw, peeled king prawns
3–4 tbsp lime juice
1 tsp finely grated lime zest
2 avocados, peeled, pitted and cut
    into bite-sized pieces
3–4 plum tomatoes, chopped
1 small red onion, finely chopped
1 small jalapeño pepper, halved,
    deseeded and finely chopped
4 tbsp chopped coriander leaves
1 tbsp ground cumin
½ tsp chilli powder

1 Cook the noodles in plenty of boiling water, according to the packet instructions. (6-9) (9-12) Drain the noodles, add the salt and toss well.

2 Meanwhile, heat 2 tablespoons of the oil in a large frying pan over a medium heat. Add the prawns and fry, turning occasionally, for 3 minutes until opaque and pink. Transfer to a large bowl, add the remaining ingredients and mix well. Stir in the noodles and mix thoroughly. Serve warm.

(6-9)

RICE NOODLES & AVOCADO PURÉE
Put 4 tablespoons of chopped, cooked noodles (drained and without the salt), 6 avocado pieces and 3 tablespoons water in a blender. Blend for 30 seconds, adding extra water 1 teaspoon at a time, until smooth. Serve warm.

(9-12)

SPICED RICE NOODLES WITH AVOCADO
Put 4 tablespoons of chopped, cooked noodles, (drained and without the salt), 6 avocado pieces, a pinch of the coriander and 3 tablespoons water in a blender. Pulse for 15 seconds, adding extra water 1 teaspoon at a time, until the mixture forms a lumpy purée. Serve warm.

Scallops with Spicy Black Bean Sauce

SERVES: 2 adults, 1 child and 1 baby
PREPARATION TIME: 35 minutes, plus 30 minutes marinating, plus at least 12 hours soaking and 1 hour 40 minutes cooking the black beans (optional), plus at least 7 hours soaking and 40 minutes cooking the brown rice
COOKING TIME: 25 minutes
STORAGE: Refrigerate the scallops for up to 1 day. Refrigerate the sauce and brown rice for up to 3 days.

....

2 tbsp toasted sesame oil
350g/12oz shelled scallops
1 onion, finely chopped
1 pepper, halved, deseeded and finely sliced
1 recipe quantity dried cooked black (turtle) beans (see page 23) or 135g/4¾oz/scant 1⅓ cups drained tinned black beans, rinsed
½ tsp fine sea salt
225g/8oz mangetout, trimmed
1 recipe quantity cooked brown rice or cooked wild rice (see page 23), to serve

FOR THE MARINADE
2 tbsp finely chopped root ginger
3 garlic cloves, finely chopped
2 tbsp tamari soy sauce or shoyu soy sauce
1 tsp toasted sesame oil

FOR THE SAUCE
240ml/8fl oz/scant 1 cup vegetable stock
3 tbsp mirin

1 To make the marinade, mix together all of the ingredients in a large, non-reactive bowl. Rinse and carefully pat the scallops dry with kitchen paper. Add the scallops to the marinade and stir well, making sure the scallops are covered in the marinade. Cover and leave to marinate in the fridge for 30 minutes.

2 To make the sauce, put the ingredients in a bowl and mix well.

3 Heat 1 tablespoon of the oil in a large frying pan over a medium-high heat until hot but not smoking. Using a slotted spoon, add the scallops to the pan and reserve the marinade. Cook for 4–5 minutes on each side until they are opaque and firm. Remove from the pan, using a slotted spoon, and transfer to a plate. (6-9) (9-12) Reduce the heat to medium and heat the remaining oil in the pan. Add the onion and pepper and cook, stirring occasionally, for 5 minutes until just tender.

4 Put the cooked black beans in a bowl with the salt. (Add the kombu, if used during cooking.) Coarsely mash the beans and add to the pan, then add the mangetout, sauce and the reserved marinade. Cook for 5 minutes until the mangetout are soft. Return the scallops to the pan and cook for 2 minutes until they have warmed through. Serve hot over the cooked brown rice.

(6-9) BROWN RICE, BLACK BEAN & MANGETOUT PURÉE
Put 4 tablespoons of the cooked brown rice and 135ml/4½fl oz/generous ½ cup boiling water in a saucepan and simmer, covered, over a low heat for 10 minutes. Add 4 mangetout and cook for a further 10 minutes until completely soft. Transfer to a blender and add 2 tablespoons of the cooked black bleans and 4 tablespoons water. Blend for 30 seconds, adding extra water 1 teaspoon at a time, until smooth. Mix in 1 teaspoon of the oil and serve warm.

(9-12) BROWN RICE, BLACK BEAN, MANGETOUT & ONION
Put 4 tablespoons of the cooked brown rice and 135ml/4½fl oz/generous ½ cup boiling water in a saucepan and simmer, covered, over a low heat for 10 minutes. Add 4 mangetout and 1 teaspoon of the onion and cook for a further 10 minutes until completely soft. Transfer to a blender and add 2 tablespoons of the cooked black beans and 4 tablespoons water. Pulse for 15 seconds, adding extra water 1 teaspoon at a time, until the mixture forms a lumpy purée. Mix in 1 teaspoon of the oil and serve warm.

Quiche is great – especially when you don't bother with the crust. We love the lift that the mustard gives this, and using yogurt instead of milk or cream is a great habit to get into. My sister Jan gave me a version of this recipe when I left home and first started cooking.

Broccoli Pecorino Quiche

SERVES: 2 adults, 1 child and 1 baby
PREPARATION TIME: 30 minutes
COOKING TIME: 40 minutes
STORAGE: Refrigerate for up to 1 day.

....

unsalted butter, for greasing
6 large eggs
350ml/12fl oz/scant 1½ cups natural
    yogurt
150g/5½oz Pecorino cheese, grated
1½ tbsp Dijon mustard
5 tbsp wholemeal spelt flour or
    wholemeal plain flour
1½ tsp finely chopped thyme leaves
½ tsp fine sea salt
175g/6oz broccoli, stems peeled and
    sliced and florets cut into bite-sized
    pieces
1 onion, finely chopped
salad, to serve
cooked brown rice pasta, millet pasta,
    quinoa pasta or buckwheat pasta,
    any shape, to serve
extra virgin olive oil, to serve

1 Preheat the oven to 180°C/350°F/gas 4 and grease a 25cm/10in pie dish with butter. In a large bowl, lightly beat the eggs together with a whisk. (9-12) Add the yogurt, Pecorino, mustard, flour, thyme and salt and whisk. (6-9) Put the broccoli and onion in the bottom of the pie dish and pour the egg mixture over the top.

2 Bake for 35–40 minutes until cooked through and the edges have browned. Serve with salad and pasta tossed with oil.

 PASTA & BROCCOLI PURÉE
Put 9 broccoli pieces in a steamer and steam, covered, for 10 minutes until completely soft. Transfer to a blender and add 4 tablespoons of chopped, cooked pasta and 3 tablespoons water. Blend for 30 seconds, adding extra water 1 teaspoon at a time, until smooth. Serve warm.

(9-12) **PASTA, BROCCOLI & ONION WITH YOGURT**
Put 6 broccoli pieces and 1 teaspoon of the onion in a steamer and steam, covered, for 10 minutes until completely soft. Transfer to a blender and add 4 tablespoons of chopped, cooked pasta and 3 tablespoons water. Pulse for 15 seconds, adding extra water 1 teaspoon at a time, until the mixture forms a lumpy purée. Mix in 2 tablespoons of the yogurt and serve warm.

Sweet potato miso mash is one of my favourite ways to eat sweet potatoes and another great way to use miso. This version of shepherd's pie combines mash with creamy lentils that are delicately sweetened with mirin.

Vegetarian Shepherd's Pie

SERVES: 2 adults, 1 child and 1 baby
PREPARATION TIME: 30 minutes, plus at least 7 hours soaking the brown lentils
COOKING TIME: 1½ hours
STORAGE: Refrigerate for up to 3 days.

....

1 recipe quantity soaked brown lentils (see page 25)
1 strip of kombu, 16 x 10cm/6¼ x 4in, finely cut with scissors (optional)
1 tomato, chopped
1 parsnip, quartered lengthways and sliced
1 carrot, quartered lengthways and sliced
1 small leek, quartered lengthways and sliced
6 garlic cloves, roughly chopped
2 tbsp chopped parsley leaves
1 tsp finely chopped thyme leaves
2 tbsp mirin
1 tsp fine sea salt
2 tbsp extra virgin olive oil, plus extra for greasing
salad, to serve

FOR THE MISO MASH
2 large potatoes, cut into chunks
1 sweet potato, cut into chunks
2 tbsp miso, any variety
6 tbsp extra virgin olive oil

1 (6-9) (9-12) Put the soaked brown lentils in a large saucepan, add 625ml/ 21½ fl oz/2½ cups water and bring to the boil over a high heat. Boil for 10 minutes, skimming any scum that rises to the surface, then turn the heat down to low and add the kombu, if using. Simmer, covered, for 25 minutes, then add the tomato, parsnip, carrot, leek, garlic, parsley and thyme and simmer, covered, for a further 10 minutes. Add the mirin, salt and oil and mix well. Remove from the heat.

2 Preheat the oven to 180°C/350°F/gas 4 and grease a 20 x 30cm/ 8 x 12in or equivalent baking dish with oil. To make the mash, put the potatoes in a steamer and steam, covered, for 20–25 minutes until soft. Remove the potatoes from the steamer and reserve 120ml/4fl oz/½ cup of the steaming water. Put the miso and the reserved steaming water in a bowl and stir until the miso has completely dissolved. Add the potatoes and oil and mash until smooth.

3 Pour the lentil mixture into the baking dish, then spread the mash on top and smooth the surface with a spatula. Bake for 25 minutes until bubbling and golden brown on top. Serve hot with salad.

(6-9) SWEET POTATO, PARSNIP & LENTIL PURÉE
Put 6 sweet potato pieces, 1 tablespoon of the parsnip, 2 tablespoons of the soaked brown lentils and 185ml/6fl oz/¾ cup water in a saucepan. Simmer, covered, over a low heat for 45 minutes until completely soft. Transfer to a blender and blend for 30 seconds, adding water 1 teaspoon at a time, until smooth. Mix in 1 teaspoon of the oil and serve warm.

(9-12) SWEET POTATO, PARSNIP, LENTIL, LEEK, GARLIC & PARSLEY
Put 6 sweet potato pieces, 1 tablespoon of the parsnip, 2 tablespoons of the soaked brown lentils, 1 teaspoon of the leek, 1 garlic piece, a pinch of the parsley and 185ml/6fl oz/¾ cup water in a saucepan. Simmer, covered, over a low heat for 45 minutes until completely soft. Transfer to a blender and pulse for 15 seconds, adding water 1 teaspoon at a time, until the mixture forms a lumpy purée. Mix in 1 teaspoon of the oil and serve warm.

Pot Pie with Cheesy Polenta

SERVES: 2 adults, 1 child and 1 baby
PREPARATION TIME: 30 minutes,
plus 10 minutes setting
COOKING TIME: 50 minutes
STORAGE: Refrigerate for up to 3 days.

....

2 tbsp extra virgin olive oil, plus extra
    for greasing
1 potato, diced
3 shallots, chopped
5 tbsp wholemeal spelt flour or
    wholemeal plain flour
375ml/13fl oz/1½ cups vegetable stock
125ml/4fl oz/½ cup natural yogurt
2 garlic cloves, crushed
2 tbsp chopped parsley leaves
1 tsp finely chopped sage leaves
½ tsp finely chopped thyme leaves
a large pinch of cayenne pepper
150g/5½oz asparagus, chopped
2 carrots, halved lengthways and sliced
100g/3½oz/⅔ cup defrosted, frozen
    peas or fresh, podded peas
90g/3¼oz/scant ⅔ cup fast-cook polenta
75g/2½oz Cheddar cheese, grated
½ tsp fine sea salt
salad, to serve

1 Preheat the oven to 200°C/400°F/gas 6 and grease a 25cm/10in pie dish with oil. Heat the oil in a large saucepan over a medium heat. (9-12) Add the potato and shallots and sprinkle the flour over the top. Cook, stirring frequently, for 5 minutes until the flour has lightly browned. Pour in the stock, then add the yogurt, garlic, parsley, sage, thyme and cayenne pepper and cook, stirring frequently, for 5 minutes until the sauce has thickened.

2 (6-9) Add the asparagus, carrots and peas to the saucepan and mix well. Pour the vegetable mix into the pie dish and level the surface with the back of a wooden spoon.

3 In a large, heavy-based saucepan, bring 435ml/15¼fl oz/1¾ cups water to the boil over a high heat. Pour the polenta in a stream, whisking continuously with a whisk until smooth. Turn the heat down to low and simmer, stirring continuously with a wooden spoon, for 5 minutes until the polenta is thick and rubbery but loose enough to spread. Remove from the heat and mix in the Cheddar and salt until well combined.

4 Spread the cheesy polenta on top of the vegetables in the pie dish and smooth the surface with a spatula. Cut a few small air holes through the polenta, using a sharp knife, and bake for 30–35 minutes until bubbling and golden brown on top. Remove from the oven and leave to set for 10 minutes. Serve hot with salad.

(6-9) **CARROT & PEA PURÉE**
Put 2½ tablespoons of the carrots in a steamer and steam, covered, for 10 minutes. Add 2½ tablespoons of the peas and steam, covered, for a further 10 minutes until completely soft. Transfer to a blender and add 3 tablespoons water. Blend for 30 seconds, adding extra water 1 teaspoon at a time, until smooth. Serve warm.

 POLENTA WITH VEGETABLES & YOGURT
Put 1 tablespoon of the carrots in a steamer and steam, covered, for 10 minutes. Add 1 tablespoon each of the asparagus, shallots and peas and steam for a further 10 minutes until completely soft. Transfer to a blender and add 2 tablespoons water. Pulse for 15 seconds, adding extra water 1 teaspoon at a time, until the mixture forms a lumpy purée. Mix in 2 tablespoons of the yogurt and serve warm with 2 tablespoons of the cooked polenta (without the cheese or salt).

We love quesadilla – and here's a different version. It's not covered with a tortilla, so you can load it up with great toppings. As long as the bottom tortilla has browned, it will hold the weight of all of the ingredients. This is good fresh and hot, or the next day without the toppings in your child's lunchbox.

Open Quesadilla with Salsa

SERVES: 2 adults, 1 child and 1 baby
PREPARATION TIME: 25 minutes, plus at least 12 hours soaking and 1 hour 40 minutes cooking the pinto beans (optional)
COOKING TIME: 30 minutes
STORAGE: Refrigerate for up to 3 days.

....

1 recipe quantity cooked dried pinto beans (see page 25) or 600g/1lb 5oz/3 cups drained tinned pinto beans, rinsed
1 tsp fine sea salt
200g/7oz/1⅓ cups frozen sweetcorn
6 wholemeal tortillas
180g/6¼oz Cheddar cheese, grated
1 avocado, peeled, pitted and chopped

FOR THE SALSA
3 tomatoes, coarsely chopped
1 small red onion, chopped
1–1½ jalapeño peppers, halved, deseeded and finely chopped
1 tbsp lemon juice
1 garlic clove, crushed
¼ tsp fine sea salt

1 (6-9) (9-18) Mix the cooked pinto beans and salt in a large bowl and set aside.

2 Put the sweetcorn in a steamer and steam, covered, for 3–4 minutes until just tender.

3 To make the salsa, put all of the ingredients in a bowl and mix well.

4 Heat a large, heavy-based frying pan over a medium-low heat until hot. Put 1 tortilla in the pan and sprinkle with 30g/1oz of the Cheddar followed by 100g/3½oz/½ cup of the cooked pinto beans. Cook for 3–4 minutes until the bottom of the tortilla has lightly browned and the cheese has melted. Slide a large spatula under the tortilla and transfer to a plate. Top with the sweetcorn, avocado and salsa and cut into slices. Repeat with the remaining tortillas and serve warm.

(6-9) **PINTO BEAN & AVOCADO PURÉE**
Put 2 tablespoons of the cooked pinto beans and 6 avocado pieces in a blender. Blend for 30 seconds, adding water 1 teaspoon at a time, until smooth. Serve warm.

(9-12) **PINTO BEAN, AVOCADO, ONION & GARLIC**
Put 1 teaspoon of the onion, a pinch of the garlic and 1 tablespoon boiling water in a frying pan and cook over a medium-high heat for 3–4 minutes until completely soft. Transfer to a blender and add 2 tablespoons of the cooked pinto beans and 6 avocado pieces. Pulse for 15 seconds, adding water 1 teaspoon at a time, until the mixture forms a lumpy purée. Serve warm.

Lentils with rice is always nice, but this is pretty
dreamy. It's lovely winter food, warm and filling with
the lentils creamy and soft on top of potatoes that are
accented with sauce and extra virgin olive oil.

Creamy Lentils on Mash

SERVES: 2 adults, 1 child and 1 baby
PREPARATION TIME: 25 minutes, plus
at least 7 hours soaking the lentils
COOKING TIME: 1 hour
STORAGE: Refrigerate for up to 3 days.

....

1 recipe quantity soaked Puy lentils
    (see page 25)
2 carrots, sliced
1 strip of kombu, 16 x 10cm/6¼ x 4in
    (optional)
120ml/4fl oz/½ cup extra virgin olive
    oil, plus extra to serve
1 onion, chopped
6 garlic cloves, chopped
100g/3½oz fresh or defrosted,
    frozen spinach, chopped
2 tsp fine sea salt
500g/1lb 2oz potatoes, diced
500g/1lb 2oz sweet potatoes, diced
3 tbsp Worcestershire sauce

1 Put the soaked Puy lentils, carrots and 800ml/28fl oz/scant 3½ cups
water in a large saucepan. Bring to the boil over a high heat, skimming
any scum that rises to the surface, then turn the heat down to low and
add the kombu, if using. Simmer, covered, for 45 minutes. Remove the
kombu from the pan, chop and set aside. (6-9) (9-12)

2 Heat 2 tablespoons of the oil in a large, heavy-based frying pan over
a medium heat. Add the onion and garlic and fry for 5 minutes until
beginning to brown. Add the onion, garlic and spinach to the lentils and
simmer, covered, for a further 10 minutes. Add the chopped kombu,
if using, and 1½ teaspoons of the salt and mix well.

3 Meanwhile, put the potatoes in a steamer and steam, covered, for 15
minutes until completely soft. Remove from the heat, transfer to a large
bowl and mash until smooth. Add the Worcestershire sauce and the
remaining oil and salt and mix well. Serve the lentils hot over the
mashed potatoes with a drizzle of oil.

(6-9)

PUY LENTIL, CARROT & SWEET POTATO PURÉE
Put 3 tablespoons of the cooked Puy lentils and
carrots, 2 tablespoons of the steamed sweet potato
and 3 tablespoons water in a blender. Blend for 30
seconds, adding extra water 1 teaspoon at a time, until
smooth. Mix in 1 teaspoon of the oil and serve warm.

(9-12)

**PUY LENTIL, CARROT, SWEET POTATO,
ONION & GARLIC STEW**
Put 5 tablespoons of the cooked Puy lentils and
carrots, 2 tablespoons of the steamed sweet potato,
1 teaspoon of the cooked onion and garlic mixture
and 3 tablespoons water in a blender. Pulse for 15
seconds, adding extra water 1 teaspoon at a time,
until the mixture forms a lumpy purée. Mix in
1 teaspoon of the oil and serve warm.

When my sister Jan and her kids arrived last July for a one-month visit, I greeted them with these. Everyone ate them so quickly that I could hardly keep up in the kitchen. They are deliciously crispy – lovely with the creamy yogurt sauce.

Lentil Fritters with Yogurt Sauce

MAKES: 12
PREPARATION TIME: 35 minutes, plus at least 12 hours soaking and 30 minutes cooking the large green lentils
COOKING TIME: 30 minutes
STORAGE: Refrigerate for up to 3 days.

....

2 large eggs
2 tsp fine sea salt
a large pinch of cayenne pepper
3 tbsp chopped parsley leaves
3 tbsp lemon juice
3 garlic cloves, crushed
1 small parsnip or carrot, grated
1 small onion, finely chopped
70–75g/2½oz frozen spinach, finely chopped
2–3 tbsp wholemeal spelt flour or wholemeal plain flour, plus extra for dusting
50g/1¾oz/½ cup porridge oats
1 recipe quantity cooked large green lentils (see page 25)
4 tbsp extra virgin olive oil, plus extra to serve
cooked pasta, any type, any shape, to serve

FOR THE YOGURT SAUCE
240ml/8fl oz/scant 1 cup natural yogurt
2 tbsp Worcestershire sauce
2 tbsp lemon juice

1 In a large mixing bowl, lightly beat the eggs together with a whisk. (6-9) (9-12) Add the salt, cayenne pepper, parsley, lemon juice, garlic, parsnip, onion, spinach, flour and oats and mix well. Add the cooked large green lentils and mix until well combined.

2 To make the sauce, put all of the ingredients in a small bowl and mix well.

3 Heat 2 tablespoons of the oil in a large, heavy-based frying pan over a medium-low heat. Working in batches, scoop the mixture by the tablespoon into your hand and shape it into a fritter. They need to be handled gently and they won't hold together well in your hand, but they do in the pan. Flip your hand over so the fritter lands in the pan and fry for 5 minutes on each side until they are crisp and golden brown. Repeat with the remaining fritters, adding the remaining oil to the pan as needed. Serve hot with the yogurt sauce and pasta tossed with oil.

(6-9) LENTIL & PARSNIP PURÉE
Put 4 tablespoons of the cooked large green lentils, 1 tablespoon of the parsnip and 3 tablespoons water in a blender. Blend for 30 seconds, adding extra water 1 teaspoon at a time, until smooth. Mix in 1 teaspoon of the oil and serve warm.

(9-12) YOGURT, LENTIL, PARSNIP & PARSLEY
Put 2 tablespoons of the yogurt, 2 tablespoons of the cooked large green lentils, 1 tablespoon of the parsnip, a pinch of the parsley and 2 tablespoons water in a blender. Pulse for 15 seconds, adding extra water 1 teaspoon at a time, until the mixture forms a lumpy purée. Mix in 1 teaspoon of the oil and serve warm.

This is the first baked stuffed squash I ever made and it's a huge hit. The flavours are perfectly balanced and it is a healthy, beautiful dish. Enjoy it as a weekend treat or serve it at festive occasions.

Baked Stuffed Squash

SERVES: 2 adults, 1 child and 1 baby
PREPARATION TIME: 30 minutes
COOKING TIME: 1 hour 10 minutes
STORAGE: Refrigerate for up to 3 days.

50g/1¾oz/⅓ cup pine nuts
1 butternut squash, halved
    and deseeded
120g/4¼oz goat's cheese, crumbled
1 fennel bulb, diced
1 leek, quartered lengthways
    and sliced
1 garlic clove, crushed
2 tbsp chopped parsley leaves
½ tsp finely chopped thyme leaves
120ml/4fl oz/½ cup extra virgin olive oil
1 tsp fine sea salt
300g/10½oz brown rice pasta, millet
    pasta, quinoa pasta or buckwheat
    pasta, any shape
avocado salad, to serve

1 Preheat the grill to medium. Put the pine nuts on a baking tray and grill for 1–2 minutes until lightly browned.

2 Preheat the oven to 200°C/400°F/gas 6. Put the squash on a baking tray and bake for 30 minutes until the flesh is soft enough to scoop out. (9-12) Meanwhile, mix the toasted pine nuts, goat's cheese, fennel, leek, garlic, parsley, thyme, 2 tablespoons of the oil and ½ teaspoon of the salt in a large bowl. (6-9) Remove the squash from the oven, scoop the flesh out with a spoon, leaving a 1cm/½in shell, and coarsely chop the flesh. Add to the toasted pine nut mixture and mix well.

3 Spoon the mixture into the squash halves and return them to the baking tray. Put any remaining filling in a small baking dish. Bake for 30–35 minutes until the top of the squash is beginning to brown and the vegetables are soft.

4 Meanwhile, cook the pasta in plenty of boiling water, according to the packet instructions. Drain the pasta and put it in a large bowl, then mix in the remaining salt and oil. Add the extra cooked filling into the pasta and mix well. Serve hot with the stuffed squash and avocado salad.

(6-9)

BAKED SQUASH, AVOCADO & PASTA PURÉE
Put 2 tablespoons of the squash flesh and 1 tablespoon water in a ramekin and bake as above for 30 minutes until completely soft. Transfer to a blender and add 2 tablespoons of chopped, cooked pasta (without the salt and oil), 2 tablespoons of avocado and 3 tablespoons water. Blend for 30 seconds, adding extra water 1 teaspoon at a time, until smooth. Serve warm.

(9-12)

PASTA WITH BAKED SQUASH, AVOCADO & VEG
Put 1 tablespoon of the squash flesh, 2 fennel pieces, 1 tablespoon of the leek and 1 tablespoon water in a ramekin and bake as above for 30 minutes until the vegetables are completely soft. Transfer to a blender and add 2 tablespoons of chopped, cooked pasta (without the salt and oil), 2 tablespoons of avocado and 3 tablespoons water. Pulse for 15 seconds, adding extra water 1 teaspoon at a time, until the mixture forms a lumpy purée. Serve warm.

When you're running out of steam, here is a great recipe to throw together. You can make this bake with kale instead of spinach. Quickly put it together, then snuggle on the sofa with your family while it quietly bakes in the oven.

Spinach & Ricotta Pasta Bake

SERVES: 2 adults, 1 child and 1 baby
PREPARATION TIME: 15 minutes
COOKING TIME: 35 minutes
STORAGE: Refrigerate for up to 3 days.

....

300g/10½oz brown rice pasta, millet pasta, quinoa pasta or buckwheat pasta, any shape
30g/1oz unsalted butter, plus extra for greasing
1 onion, finely chopped
250g/9oz fresh or defrosted, frozen baby spinach leaves, finely chopped
225g/8oz ricotta cheese
1 tsp chopped rosemary leaves
½ tsp finely chopped thyme leaves
4 tbsp extra virgin olive oil
1¼ tsp fine sea salt
300g/10½oz drained, bottled or tinned artichoke hearts in water or oil, chopped

1 Preheat the oven to 180°C/350°F/gas 4 and grease a large baking dish with butter. Cook the pasta in plenty of boiling water for half the time directed by the packet instructions. (6-9) (9-12) Drain well and set aside.

2 Meanwhile, heat the butter in a large, heavy-based frying pan over a medium heat until melted. Add the onion and cook, stirring occasionally, for 5 minutes until beginning to brown. Remove from the heat and mix in the pasta, spinach, ricotta, rosemary, thyme, oil, salt and 290ml/10fl oz/ 1 cup + 2 tablespoons water and stir until well combined and the ricotta has melted.

3 Arrange the artichokes over the bottom of the baking dish, cover with the spinach and pasta mixture and smooth the surface with a spatula. Bake for 30 minutes until bubbling and beginning to brown. Serve hot.

(6-9) ARTICHOKE & PASTA PURÉE
Leave 3 tablespoons of the cooked pasta to cook for the full time directed by the packet instructions. Drain well and chop. Transfer to a blender and add 6 artichoke pieces and 3 tablespoons water. Blend for 30 seconds, adding extra water 1 teaspoon at a time, until smooth. Mix in 1 teaspoon of the oil and serve warm.

 BUTTER-FRIED ARTICHOKE PASTA
Leave 3 tablespoons of the cooked pasta to cook for the full time directed by the packet instructions. Drain well and chop. Heat 1 teaspoon of the butter in a heavy-based frying pan until melted. Add the pasta, 6 artichoke pieces and 1 teaspoon of the onion and cook for 10 minutes until completely soft. Transfer to a blender and add 3 tablespoons water. Pulse for 15 seconds, adding extra water 1 teaspoon at a time, until the mixture forms a lumpy purée. Serve warm.

Here is my new love instead of risotto. The flavours are absolutely wonderful and I don't have to stand over the hob. Peas, which are often a favourite with children because they are a great finger food, are sweet and packed with nutrients like antioxidants.

Baked Lemon & Pea Rice

SERVES: 2 adults, 1 child and 1 baby
PREPARATION TIME: 20 minutes, plus at least 7 hours soaking
COOKING TIME: 45 minutes
STORAGE: Refrigerate for up to 3 days.

....

200g/7oz/1 cup brown
    Arborio or risotto rice
1 tbsp natural yogurt or kefir, for soaking
4 tbsp extra virgin olive oil
1 leek, quartered lengthways and sliced
zest of 1 lemon
500ml/17fl oz/2 cups vegetable stock
120g/4¼oz/heaped ¾ cup defrosted,
    frozen peas or fresh, podded peas
4 tbsp chopped parsley leaves
50g/1¾oz Parmesan cheese, grated
2 tbsp lemon juice

1 Put the rice and yogurt in a large bowl and cover generously with warm water. Leave to soak, covered, for 7 hours or overnight at room temperature. Drain well. (6-9) (9-12)

2 Preheat the oven to 200°C/400°F/gas 6. Pour the oil into a large casserole dish and heat a large saucepan over a medium-high heat until hot. Add the soaked rice to the pan and cook, stirring continuously, for 5 minutes, or until dry. Transfer the rice to the casserole dish and stir well, making sure the rice is thoroughly coated in the oil. Mix in the leek and ¾ of the lemon zest, then pour in the stock and stir well. Bake for 35–40 minutes until the rice is soft but still has a slight bite and there is only a little stock left in the casserole dish.

3 Remove the casserole dish from the oven and stir in the peas, 3 tablespoons of the parsley, ¾ of the Parmesan and the lemon juice. Serve warm, sprinkled with the remaining lemon zest, parsley and Parmesan.

(6-9) ARBORIO RICE & PEA PURÉE
Put 4 tablespoons of the soaked rice in a saucepan, add 375ml/13fl oz/ 1½ cups boiling water and simmer, covered, over a low heat for 50 minutes. Add 2 tablespoons of the peas and simmer, covered, for a further 10 minutes until completely soft. Transfer to a blender and add 3 tablespoons water. Blend for 30 seconds, adding extra water 1 teaspoon at a time, until smooth. Mix in 1 teaspoon of the oil and serve warm.

(9-12) ARBORIO RICE WITH PEAS, LEEKS & PARSLEY
Put 4 tablespoons of the soaked rice in a saucepan, add 375ml/13fl oz/ 1½ cups boiling water and simmer, covered, over a low heat for 50 minutes. Add 2 tablespoons of the peas, 1 tablespoon of the leek and 1 teaspoon of the parsley and simmer, covered, for a further 10 minutes until completely soft. Transfer to a blender and add 3 tablespoons water. Pulse for 15 seconds, adding extra water 1 teaspoon at a time, until the mixture forms a lumpy purée. Mix in 1 teaspoon of the oil and serve warm.

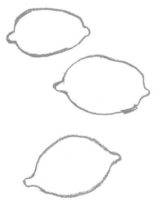

Stuffing is a good way to introduce grains other than rice into your cooking and your kids. Just scoop the raw courgettes out and fill with this crunchy, tasty mix of millet, Parmesan and seeds roasted in tamari.

Courgette Baked with Toasted Seeds

SERVES: 2 adults, 1 child and 1 baby
PREPARATION TIME: 25 minutes, plus at least 7 hours soaking and 20 minutes cooking the millet
COOKING TIME: 30 minutes
STORAGE: Refrigerate for up to 3 days.

....

10g/¼oz arame (optional)
2 tbsp sunflower seeds
2 tbsp pumpkin seeds
1 tbsp sesame seeds
1 tsp tamari soy sauce or shoyu soy sauce
a large pinch of cayenne pepper
4 courgettes, halved
1 egg
1 tbsp extra virgin olive oil, plus extra for greasing
½ recipe quantity cooked millet, cooked quinoa or cooked brown rice (see page 22)
2½ tbsp natural yogurt
30g/1oz Parmesan cheese, grated
½ tsp fine sea salt

1 Preheat the oven to 200°C/400°F/gas 6 and grease a large baking dish with oil. Using your fingertips, crush the arame in a small bowl, if using. Add 4 tablespoons boiling water and leave to soak for 10 minutes. Mix together the seeds, tamari and cayenne pepper in a small bowl.

2 Scoop the flesh out of the courgette halves with a spoon leaving a 1cm/½in shell, then coarsely chop the flesh. **(6-9)** **(9-12)** Discard the flesh. In a large bowl, lightly beat the egg with a whisk. Add the arame, if using, oil, cooked millet, yogurt, Parmesan and salt and mix well. Spoon the mixture evenly into the hollowed out courgette halves and sprinkle the seed mix on top. Put the courgette halves in the baking dish and bake for 30 minutes until the courgettes are just soft and the topping is browned. Serve hot.

(6-9) **MILLET & COURGETTE PURÉE**
Put 4 tablespoons of the cooked millet and 135ml/4½fl oz/generous ½ cup boiling water in a saucepan and simmer, covered, over a low heat for 20 minutes until completely soft. Put 3 tablespoons of the courgette flesh in a steamer and steam, covered, for 10 minutes until completely soft. Transfer to a blender and add the cooked millet and 3 tablespoons water. Blend for 30 seconds, adding extra water 1 teaspoon at a time, until smooth. Mix in 1 teaspoon of the oil and serve warm.

 MILLET & COURGETTE WITH YOGURT
Put 4 tablespoons of the cooked millet and 135ml/4½fl oz/generous ½ cup boiling water in a saucepan and simmer, covered, over a low heat for 20 minutes until completely soft. Put 3 tablespoons of the courgette flesh in a steamer and steam, covered, for 10 minutes until completely soft. Transfer to a blender and add the cooked millet, 2 tablespoons of the yogurt and 2 tablespoons water. Pulse for 15 seconds, adding extra water 1 teaspoon at a time, until the mixture forms a lumpy purée. Serve warm.

This is so creamy with the melting feta. Everything comes together so much that you can't even tell that it's millet. I find bakes are another easy way to try a grain other than rice or pasta.

Millet & Mung Bean Bake

SERVES: 2 adults, 1 child and 1 baby
PREPARATION TIME: 30 minutes, plus at least 12 hours soaking and 55 minutes cooking the mung beans (optional), plus at least 7 hours soaking and 20 minutes cooking the millet
COOKING TIME: 30 minutes
STORAGE: Refrigerate for up to 3 days.

....

4 tbsp extra virgin olive oil, plus extra for greasing
100g/3½oz broccoli, cut into bite-sized florets
100g/3½oz/⅔ cup defrosted, frozen peas or fresh, podded peas
1 leek, halved lengthways and sliced
200g/7oz feta cheese, diced
2 tbsp Worcestershire sauce
1 tsp fine sea salt
1 recipe quantity cooked mung beans (see page 24) or 360g/12¾/2 cups drained tinned mung beans, rinsed
1 recipe quantity cooked millet (see page 22)
40g/1½oz unsalted butter
60g/2¼oz/scant ⅔ cup dried wholemeal breadcrumbs
salad, to serve

1 Preheat the oven to 200°C/400°F/gas 6 and grease a large baking dish with oil. (6-9) (9-12) In a large bowl, mix together the oil, broccoli, peas, leek, feta, Worcestershire sauce, salt and 125ml/4fl oz/½ cup water. Add the cooked mung beans and cooked millet and mix well. (Chop and add the kombu, if used during cooking.) Put the mixture in the baking dish and smooth the top with the back of a wooden spoon.

2 Heat the butter in a saucepan over a low heat until melted, then remove from the heat. Add the breadcrumbs and mix until well combined. Sprinkle the buttered breadcrumbs over the top of the millet and mung bean mixture and bake for 25–30 minutes until bubbling and lightly browned. Serve hot with salad.

(6-9) MILLET, MUNG BEAN, BROCCOLI & PEA PURÉE
Finely chop 3 broccoli pieces. Put the broccoli, 2 tablespoons of the cooked millet, 1 tablespoon of the cooked mung beans, 1 tablespoon of the peas and 3 tablespoons water in a ramekin. Bake as above for 20 minutes until the vegetables are completely soft. Transfer to a blender and blend for 30 seconds, adding extra water 1 teaspoon at a time, until smooth. Mix in 1 teaspoon of the oil and serve warm.

(9-12) MILLET, MUNG BEAN, BROCCOLI, PEA & LEEK BAKE
Finely chop 3 broccoli pieces and 1 teaspoon of the leek. Put the broccoli and leek, 2 tablespoons of the cooked millet, 1 tablespoon of the cooked mung beans, 1 tablespoon of the peas and 3 tablespoons water in a ramekin. Bake as above for 20 minutes until the vegetables are completely soft. Transfer to a blender and pulse for 15 seconds, adding extra water 1 teaspoon at a time, until the mixture forms a lumpy purée. Mix in 1 teaspoon of the oil and serve warm.

I love the idea of lasagne, but I'm not keen on béchamel and didn't want to have to make tomato sauce because lasagne already takes a lot of time. Here is the first recipe I created for this book, with the help of my friend Anita. We gathered some of my favourite ingredients and put together this amazing dish.

Roasted Vegetable Lasagne

SERVES: 4 adults and 4 children
PREPARATION TIME: 1 hour
COOKING TIME: 1 hour 10 minutes
STORAGE: Refrigerate for up to 3 days.

....

1kg/2lb 4oz plum tomatoes, thickly
    sliced
135ml/4½fl oz/generous ½ cup olive
    oil, plus extra for greasing
3 tbsp chopped parsley leaves
1 tbsp chopped oregano leaves or
    1 tsp dried oregano
1 tsp fincly chopped thyme leaves or
    1 tsp dried thyme
300g/10½oz drained, bottled
    or tinned artichoke hearts in water
    or oil, thinly sliced lengthways
1 small yellow pepper, halved,
    deseeded and thinly sliced
2 red onions, halved and thinly sliced
1 small courgette, thinly sliced
1 tsp salt
9 wholemeal spelt lasagne sheets
    or wholemeal lasagne sheets
500g/1lb 2oz mozzarella balls,
    drained and thinly sliced
115g/4oz/scant ¼ cup drained capers
    in salt or brine, rinsed
150g/5½oz drained, bottled or tinned,
    pitted black olives, chopped
4 garlic cloves, thinly sliced
55g/2oz/heaped 1 cup grated
    Parmesan cheese
avocado salad, to serve

1 Preheat the oven to 250°C/500°F/gas 9 and grease one baking dish and one large baking dish with oil. Put the tomatoes in the baking dish and drizzle 3 tablespoons of the oil over the top. Sprinkle with the parsley, oregano and thyme and toss gently but thoroughly. Put the artichokes, pepper, onions and courgette in the large baking dish, drizzle with 5 tablespoons of the oil and toss gently. Put both baking dishes in the oven and bake for 30 minutes until the vegetables are soft and beginning to brown. Remove from the oven then set aside to cool. (6-9) (9-12)

2 Turn the oven down to 200°C/400°F/gas 6. Transfer the roasted vegetables to a large bowl, add the salt and toss well.

3 Drizzle the remaining oil over the bottom of the large baking dish, then spread ⅓ of the roasted tomatoes evenly over the bottom, followed by 3 lasagne sheets, ¼ of the mozzarella, ⅓ of the roasted vegetable mixture, ⅓ of the capers, ¼ of the olives and ⅓ of the garlic. Repeat the layers twice, then sprinkle the Parmesan and the remaining mozzarella and olives evenly over the top.

4 Bake for 40 minutes until the top is bubbling and golden brown. Serve hot with avocado salad.

(6-9) ARTICHOKE, COURGETTE & AVOCADO PURÉE
Put 3 tablespoons of the roasted artichokes, 2 tablespoons of the roasted courgette, 2 tablespoons of avocado and 3 tablespoons water in a blender. Blend for 30 seconds, adding extra water 1 teaspoon at a time, until smooth. Serve warm.

(9-12) ROASTED ARTICHOKE, COURGETTE, ONION & AVOCADO
Put 2 tablespoons each of the roasted artichokes, courgette, onions and avocado and 3 tablespoons water in a blender. Pulse for 15 seconds, adding extra water 1 teaspoon at a time, until the mixture forms a lumpy purée. Serve warm.

Teriyaki Tofu

MAKES: 12 skewers
PREPARATION TIME: 50 minutes, plus 1 hour marinating, plus at least 7 hours soaking and 40 minutes cooking the red Camargue rice
COOKING TIME: 25 minutes
STORAGE: Refrigerate for up to 3 days.

....

6 tbsp extra virgin olive oil
175g/6oz tofu or tempeh, cut into 24 bite-sized pieces
1 small red pepper, halved, deseeded and cut into 12 pieces
12 button mushrooms
1 courgette, cut into 12 slices
1 small fennel bulb, cut into 12 pieces
3 shallots, quartered
1 tsp fine sea salt
1 recipe quantity cooked red Camargue rice or cooked brown rice (see page 23)

FOR THE MARINADE
1½ tbsp cornflour, ground arrowroot or crushed kuzu
1½ tbsp tamari soy sauce or shoyu soy sauce
4 tbsp mirin
1 tbsp grated root ginger

1 Grease a shallow baking dish with 1 tablespoon of the oil. To make the marinade, mix the cornflour and 1½ tablespoons cold water together to make a smooth paste in a bowl. Put the cornflour mixture, 330ml/11¼fl oz/1⅓ cups water and all of the remaining ingredients for the marinade in a saucepan. Cook over a medium heat for 3–5 minutes, stirring continuously, until the marinade thickens. Remove the pan from the heat and set aside to cool for 10 minutes. Add a little water if the marinade becomes too thick to pour.

2 (6-9) (9-12) Thread 1 piece of the tofu, 1 piece of pepper, a mushroom and 1 piece each of the courgette, fennel and shallots onto a metal or bamboo skewer. Finish with another piece of the tofu and repeat with the remaining skewers. Put the skewers in the baking dish and spoon the marinade over the top. Leave to marinate, covered, for 1 hour at room temperature.

3 Preheat the grill to medium-high. Reserve the marinade and grill the skewers for 20 minutes, turning once and brushing with more of the marinade, until the vegetables and tofu are beginning to brown. Mix the salt, the remaining marinade and the remaining oil into the cooked red Camargue rice and serve warm with the skewers.

(6-9) **RED RICE & COURGETTE PURÉE**
Put 4 tablespoons of the cooked red Camargue rice and 135ml/4½fl oz/generous ½ cup boiling water in a saucepan and simmer, covered, over a low heat for 10 minutes. Add 6 courgette pieces and simmer, covered, for a further 10 minutes until completely soft. Transfer to a blender and add 3 tablespoons water. Blend for 30 seconds, adding extra water 1 teaspoon at a time, until smooth. Mix in 1 teaspoon of the oil and serve warm.

(9-12) **RED RICE WITH COURGETTE & FENNEL**
Put 4 tablespoons of the cooked red Camargue rice and 135ml/4½fl oz/generous ½ cup boiling water in a saucepan and simmer, covered, over a low heat for 10 minutes. Add 3 pieces each of the courgette and fennel and simmer, covered, for a futher 10 minutes until completely soft. Transfer to a blender and add 3 tablespoons water. Pulse for 15 seconds, adding extra water 1 teaspoon at a time, until the mixture forms a lumpy purée. Mix in 1 teaspoon of the oil and serve warm.

Hand rolls are the easiest way to eat sushi because even children can roll them, hold them and eat them. You can pile the ingredients onto the table and let everyone make their own – beautiful triangles bursting with colour and flavour.

Nori Hand Rolls

MAKES: 20
PREPARATION TIME: 20 minutes, plus at least 7 hours soaking and 40 minutes cooking the brown sushi rice
COOKING TIME: 5 minutes
STORAGE: Refrigerate for up to 3 days.

....

10 asparagus, woody ends removed and halved
40 green beans, trimmed
1 tsp fine sea salt
1 recipe quantity cooked brown sushi rice or brown short grain rice (see page 23)
10 nori sheets, halved lengthways
½ tbsp wasabi (optional)
1 beetroot, grated
50g/1¾oz sprouts such as alfalfa, broccoli or mung (optional)

FOR THE SAUCE
2 avocados, peeled, pitted and mashed
2 tbsp mayonnaise

1 (6-9) (9-12) Put the asparagus and green beans in a steamer and steam, covered, for 5 minutes until the vegetables are cooked but still slightly crunchy. Add the salt to the cooked brown sushi rice and mix well.

2 To make the sauce, mix together the avocados and mayonnaise in a bowl until smooth.

3 To make a hand roll, spread 1 tablespoon of the sauce diagonally down the centre of one nori sheet, then add a little wasabi on top, if using. Put 1 tablespoon of the cooked brown sushi rice, 1 piece of asparagus, 2 green beans and 1 tablespoon each of the beetroot and sprouts, if using, on top of the sauce. Take the nori sheet in your hand and roll into a cone shape. Repeat with the remaining ingredients and serve.

(6-9) **GREEN BEAN, AVOCADO & RICE PURÉE**
Put 4 tablespoons of the cooked brown sushi rice and 135ml/4½fl oz/ generous ½ cup boiling water in a saucepan and simmer, covered, over a low heat for 10 minutes. Add 4 green beans and cook, covered, for a further 10 minutes until completely soft. Transfer to a blender and add 2 tablespoons of the avocado and 3 tablespoons water. Blend for 30 seconds, adding extra water 1 teaspoon at a time, until smooth. Serve warm.

(9-12) **VEGETABLES, AVOCADO, SPROUTS, BEETROOT & RICE**
Put 4 tablespoons of the cooked brown sushi rice and 135ml/4½fl oz/ generous ½ cup boiling water in a saucepan and simmer, covered, over a low heat for 10 minutes. Add 2 green beans and 1 asparagus piece and cook for a further 10 minutes until completely soft. Transfer to a blender and add 2 tablespoons of the avocado, 1 tablespoon each of the beetroot and sprouts, if using, and 3 tablespoons water. Pulse for 15 seconds, adding extra water 1 teaspoon at a time, until the mixture forms a lumpy purée. Serve warm.

Cheesy Bake with Mole

SERVES: 4 adults and 4 children
PREPARATION TIME: 1 hour, plus at
least 7 hours soaking and 20 minutes
cooking the red quinoa, plus at least
7 hours soaking and 40 minutes
cooking the red Camargue rice
COOKING TIME: 1 hour 20 minutes
STORAGE: Refrigerate for up to 1 day.

....

unsalted butter, for greasing
20g/¾oz dried porcini mushrooms
100g/3½oz/1 cup pecans
100g/3½oz/1 cup walnuts
5 large eggs
1 onion, finely chopped
2 garlic cloves, crushed
4 tbsp parsley leaves, chopped
2 tsp finely chopped thyme leaves
1 tsp finely chopped sage leaves
½ tsp fine sea salt
250g/9oz ricotta cheese
250g/9oz Cheddar cheese, grated
½ recipe quantity cooked red quinoa
    or quinoa (see page 22)
½ recipe quantity cooked red Camargue
    rice or cooked brown rice
    (see page 23)
avocado, cucumber and tomato salad,
    to serve
mayonnaise, to serve

FOR THE MOLE

2 tsp extra virgin olive oil
1 small onion, finely chopped
1 tbsp cocoa powder
1 tsp ground cumin
1 tsp ground coriander
1 garlic clove, finely chopped
5 dried bird's-eye chillies, finely
    chopped
280g/10oz tomatoes, diced
¼ tsp fine sea salt

1 Preheat the grill to medium and grease a 23 x 13cm/9 x 5in loaf tin with butter. Line the loaf tin with baking parchment and grease again. Soak the porcini mushrooms in 280ml/10fl oz/generous 1 cup water for 20 minutes until softened. Drain, squeeze out any excess water and chop. Put the nuts on a baking tray and grill for 1–2 minutes until lightly browned. Remove from the grill and roughly chop the nuts.

2 Preheat the oven to 190°C/375°F/gas 5. In a large bowl, lightly beat the eggs together with a whisk. (6-9) (9-12) Add the onion, garlic, parsley, thyme, sage, salt, ricotta, Cheddar, porcini mushrooms, toasted nuts, cooked red quinoa and cooked red Camargue rice and mix well. Spoon the mixture into the loaf tin, smooth the surface with the back of a metal spoon and bake for 1 hour 15 minutes until risen, browned and cracked.

3 Meanwhile, make the mole. Heat the oil in a heavy-based frying pan over a medium heat. Add the onion and fry for 5 minutes until soft. Mix in all of the remaining ingredients and bring to the boil over a high heat, then turn the heat down to low and simmer, covered, for 15 minutes, stirring occasionally, until the vegetables are soft. Remove the bake from the oven and leave to cool in the tin for 10 minutes. Turn the bake out of the tin, then transfer to a serving plate, right-side up. Serve hot with the mole (for adults), and an avocado, cucumber and tomato salad with mayonnaise.

(6-9) RED RICE, RED QUINOA & AVOCADO PURÉE
Put 2 tablespoons of the cooked red Camargue rice, 2 tablespoons of the cooked red quinoa and 135ml/4½fl oz/generous ½ cup boiling water in a saucepan and simmer, covered, for 20 minutes until completely soft. Transfer to a blender and add 6 avocado pieces and 3 tablespoons water. Blend for 30 seconds, adding extra water 1 teaspoon at a time, until smooth. Serve warm.

(9-12) RED RICE & RED QUINOA WITH AVOCADO, ONION & PARSLEY
Put 2 tablespoons of the cooked red Camargue rice, 2 tablespoons of the cooked red quinoa, 1 teaspoon each of the onion and parsley and 135ml/4½fl oz/generous ½ cup boiling water in a saucepan and simmer, covered, for 20 minutes until completely soft. Transfer to a blender and add 6 avocado pieces and 3 tablespoons water. Pulse for 15 seconds, adding extra water 1 teaspoon at a time, until the mixture forms a lumpy purée. Serve warm.

White food is generally so unhealthy that I decided to try to make white food that is actually good for you. I took everything white I had in the kitchen and made this soup.

White Vegetable Soup

SERVES: 4 adults and 4 children
PREPARATION TIME: 25 minutes, plus at least 12 hours soaking and 1 hour 40 minutes cooking the haricot beans (optional)
COOKING TIME: 40 minutes
STORAGE: Refrigerate for up to 3 days, or freeze for up to 3 months.

....

2 tbsp extra virgin olive oil, plus extra
   to serve
1 onion, chopped
5 garlic cloves, quartered
500g/1lb 2oz potatoes, chopped
½ recipe quantity cooked dried haricot
   beans (see page 24) or 200g/7oz/
   1 cup drained tinned haricot beans,
   rinsed
250g/9oz cauliflower, cut into
   bite-sized florets
½ tbsp fine sea salt
hot pepper sauce, to serve
salad, to serve
wholemeal bread, to serve

1 (6-9) (9-12) Heat the oil in a large, heavy-based saucepan over a medium heat. Add the onion and cook, stirring occasionally, for 5 minutes until beginning to brown, then turn the heat up to high. Add the garlic, potatoes and 480ml/16fl oz/scant 2 cups water. Bring to a simmer and cook, covered, over a low heat for a further 20 minutes. Add the cooked haricot beans and cauliflower and cook for another 10 minutes until the cauliflower is soft. (Chop and add the kombu, if used during cooking.) Stir in the salt and remove the pan from the heat.

2 Transfer ½ of the soup to a blender and blend until creamy. Return the blended soup to the pan, reheating if necessary. Serve hot, drizzled with hot pepper sauce, and with salad, wholemeal bread and oil.

(6-9) HARICOT BEANS & CAULIFLOWER PURÉE
Put 6 cauliflower pieces in a steamer and steam, covered, for 10 minutes until completely soft. Transfer to a blender and add 3 tablespoons of the cooked haricot beans and 3 tablespoons water. Blend for 30 seconds, adding extra water 1 teaspoon at a time, until smooth. Mix in 1 teaspoon of the oil and serve warm.

(9-12) HARICOT BEANS, CAULIFLOWER & GARLIC
Put 6 cauliflower pieces and 1 garlic piece in a steamer and steam, covered, for 10 minutes until completely soft. Transfer to a blender and add 3 tablespoons of the cooked haricot beans and 3 tablespoons water. Pulse for 15 seconds, adding extra water 1 teaspoon at a time, until the mixture forms a lumpy purée. Mix in 1 teaspoon of the oil and serve warm.

This is a simple dinner, but it has great flavours. Toasted sesame seeds, miso, ginger and a hint of chilli make a mouth-watering mix. The water chestnuts add crunchy texture to the soft noodles and there is plenty of sauce to go around.

Spicy Soba with Pak Choi

SERVES: 2 adults, 1 child and 1 baby
PREPARATION TIME: 30 minutes
COOKING TIME: 15 minutes
STORAGE: Refrigerate for up to 3 days.

....

300g/10½oz 100% buckwheat soba
   noodles or brown rice noodles
2 tbsp sesame seeds
5 tbsp white miso
5 tbsp mirin
1 tbsp finely chopped root ginger
4 tbsp sesame oil
3 spring onions, white parts finely
   chopped and green parts cut
   into rings
200g/7oz pak choi, roughly chopped
150g/5½oz broccoli, cut into bite-sized
   pieces
100g/3½oz water chestnuts, halved
a large pinch of crushed chilli

1 Cook the noodles in plenty of boiling water, according to the packet instructions. Gradually add the noodles to the pan to keep the water at boiling point. Stir gently to prevent the noodles from sticking to the bottom of the pan. Drain, then rinse the noodles under cold running water to prevent further cooking and to make sure the noodles don't stick together. Drain again.

2 Meanwhile, heat a large frying pan over a medium heat until hot. Add the sesame seeds and dry-fry for 3–4 minutes until beginning to brown. Remove from the heat and set aside. Mix the white miso, mirin and ginger in a bowl.

3 Heat the oil in a wok or large frying pan over a medium-high heat. Add the white part of the spring onions and stir-fry for 2 minutes. Add the pak choi, broccoli and 185ml/6fl oz/¾ cup water and cook for 5–7 minutes until just tender. Remove from the heat, then stir in the toasted sesame seeds, white miso mixture, water chestnuts and crushed chilli. Serve hot with the noodles and the green part of the spring onions sprinkled over the top.

 BUCKWHEAT NOODLE & BROCCOLI PURÉE
Heat 1 teaspoon of the oil and 3 tablespoons water in a frying pan. Add 6 broccoli pieces and cook, covered, over a low heat for 10 minutes until completely soft. Transfer to a blender and add 3 tablespoons of chopped, cooked noodles and 3 tablespoons water. Blend for 30 seconds, adding extra water 1 teaspoon at a time, until smooth. Serve warm.

 BUCKWHEAT NOODLES, PAK CHOI, BROCCOLI & SPRING ONION
Heat 1 teaspoon of the oil and 3 tablespoons water in a frying pan. Add 1 tablespoon of the pak choi, 6 broccoli pieces and 1 teaspoon of the white part of the spring onions and cook, covered, over a low heat for 10 minutes until completely soft. Transfer to a blender and add 3 tablespoons of chopped, cooked noodles and 3 tablespoons water. Pulse for 15 seconds, adding extra water 1 teaspoon at a time, until the mixture forms a lumpy purée. Serve warm.

chapter four
baked treats

We finish off with the absolute joy of baking.
Here are breakfast breads, healthy snacks, bakes
and cakes, pies and puddings – and fruits galore.
Not a huge fan of dessert, I make my sweet
treats with ingredients like wholemeal flour, rice
malt syrup, fruits or vegetables. But you'd never
know it – guests never guess that my brownies
contain sweet potatoes and who cares if pie is
made with wholemeal pastry?

This chapter is not about serving desserts to
your children every day – and certainly not to
a baby. But it will provide you with methods for
cooking and baking fruits, like Apple & Blueberry
Bake, which is great for snacking or adding to
lunchboxes, and means you've got Baked Apple
& Buckwheat Purée for a 6–9 month old or Baked
Apple & Blueberry for a 9–12 month old.

Breakfast Bread

MAKES: 1 loaf (about 16 slices)
PREPARATION TIME: 20 minutes, plus at least 3 hours rising
COOKING TIME: 35 minutes
STORAGE: Store in an airtight container for up to 2 days, then refrigerate for up to 3 days or slice and freeze for up to 3 months.

....

360g/12¾oz/3 cups wholemeal spelt flour or wholemeal plain flour, plus extra for dusting
100g/3½oz/1 cup porridge oats or any flaked wholemeal grain, such as millet, barley or buckwheat
120g/4¼oz/⅔ cup dried unsulphured apricots, ¾ halved and ¼ finely chopped
3 tbsp sunflower seeds
3 tbsp linseeds
2 tbsp sesame seeds
2 tsp fine sea salt
2 tsp dried active yeast
4 tbsp rice malt syrup or 3 tbsp cane sugar
2 tbsp sunflower oil, plus extra for greasing
2½ tbsp natural yogurt
unsalted butter, for greasing and to serve

1 Mix the flour, oats, apricots, seeds and salt in a large bowl. Make a well in the centre of the mixture and add the yeast and rice malt syrup. Pour in 200ml/7fl oz/scant 1 cup warm water to dissolve the yeast and rice malt syrup.

2 Add the oil and yogurt and bring the dough together with a wooden spoon. Turn the dough out onto a work surface and knead for 10 minutes until smooth and elastic, adding a little more flour if the dough sticks to your hands or work surface. Rinse and dry the mixing bowl, then lightly grease it with oil. Return the dough to the mixing bowl and turn until completely coated in oil. Leave to rise for 1½–2 hours until doubled in size.

3 Grease a 23 x 13cm/9 x 5in loaf tin with butter. Turn the dough out onto a work surface and punch it down to get rid of any air bubbles. Knead for 1 minute, then shape into a log the length of the tin. Put the dough in the tin and leave to rise for another 1½–2 hours until doubled in size.

4 Preheat the oven to 220°C/425°F/gas 7. Bake for 15 minutes, then turn the heat down to 190°C/375°F/gas 5 and bake for a further 20 minutes until firm to the touch. Remove from the oven and leave to cool for 15 minutes, then turn out of the tin, transfer to a wire rack and leave to cool. Serve warm or toasted with butter.

APRICOT PURÉE

Put 8 apricot halves and 150ml/5fl oz/scant ⅔ cup water in a saucepan. Bring to the boil over a high heat, then turn the heat down to low and simmer, covered, for 15 minutes until completely soft. Leave to cool slightly, then transfer to a blender and blend for 30 seconds, adding water 1 teaspoon at a time, until smooth. Serve warm.

APRICOT & OAT MIX

Put 8 apricot halves, 4 tablespoons of the oats, ½ tablespoon of the yogurt and 240ml/8fl oz/scant 1 cup water in a saucepan. Leave to soak, covered, for 7 hours or overnight at room temperature. Bring to the boil over a high heat, then turn the heat down to low and simmer, covered, for 15 minutes, stirring occasionally, until completely soft. Transfer to a blender and pulse for 15 seconds, adding water 1 teaspoon at a time, until the mixture forms a lumpy purée. Serve warm.

Banana bread is a great way to use up old bananas. Made with wholemeal flour and walnuts, this has evolved from my mom's recipe from when we were kids. I remember waiting with my sisters and brother to lick the bowl and spatula.

Banana Walnut Bread

MAKES: 1 loaf (about 16 slices)
PREPARATION TIME: 30 minutes
COOKING TIME: 1 hour
STORAGE: Store in an airtight container for up to 2 days, then refrigerate for up to 3 days or slice and freeze for up to 3 months.

....

120g/4¼oz/1 cup wholemeal spelt flour or wholemeal plain flour
120g/4¼oz/1 cup white spelt flour or white plain flour, plus extra for dusting
2 tsp baking powder
½ tsp fine sea salt
125g/4½oz unsalted butter, at room temperature, plus extra for greasing and to serve
150g/5½oz/¾ cup cane sugar
2 large eggs
125ml/4fl oz/½ cup oat milk, rice milk or water
1 tsp vanilla extract
2 ripe or overripe bananas, mashed
50g/1¾oz/½ cup walnuts, chopped

1 Preheat the oven to 180°C/350°F/gas 4 and grease and flour a 23 x 13cm/9 x 5in loaf tin.

2 Mix the flours, baking powder and salt in a bowl. Put the butter and sugar in a large mixing bowl and beat, using an electric mixer, for 5 minutes until creamy. Add the eggs, one at a time, beating well after each addition. **(6-9) (9-12)** Add the oat milk, vanilla extract, bananas, walnuts and the flour mixture and beat for 30 seconds until just combined, but take care not to overmix.

3 Pour the mixture into the loaf tin and level the surface, using a clean knife. Bake for 55 minutes–1 hour until firm to the touch, browned and a skewer inserted into the centre comes out clean. Remove from the oven and leave to cool for 20 minutes. Run a knife around the edge of the loaf, then turn out of the tin, transfer to a wire rack and leave to cool. Serve warm or at room temperature, plain or with butter.

(6-9) BANANA PURÉE
Put ¼ of the mashed banana and 2 tablespoons water in a blender. Blend for 30 seconds, adding extra water 1 teaspoon at a time, until smooth. Serve warm or at room temperature.

 BANANA & OAT MILK MIX
Put ¼ of the mashed banana and 2 tablespoons of the oat milk in a bowl and mix until well combined. Serve warm or at room temperature.

Corn bread makes a tasty change from flour-based snacks and is good warm or cold, plain or toasted with butter. Apricots add a nice touch here, giving extra sweetness and goodness. Make sure you buy organic apricots, which are unsulphured.

Apricot Corn Bread

MAKES: 1 loaf (about 16 slices)
PREPARATION TIME: 25 minutes
COOKING TIME: 1 hour and 5 minutes
STORAGE: Store in airtight container for up to 2 days, then refrigerate for up to 3 days.

....

320g/11¼oz/scant 2¼ cups cornmeal or fast-cook polenta
120g/4¼oz/1 cup white spelt flour or white plain flour
60g/2¼oz/½ cup brown rice flour
200g/7oz/1 cup cane sugar
2 tsp bicarbonate of soda
1 tsp fine sea salt
60g/2¼oz unsalted butter or 60ml/ 2fl oz/¼ cup sunflower oil, plus extra for greasing
2 large eggs
240ml/8fl oz/scant 1 cup natural yogurt
150g/5½oz/heaped ¾ cup dried, unsulphured apricots, finely chopped

1 Preheat the oven to 170°C/325°F/gas 3. Grease a 23 x 13cm/9 x 5in loaf tin with butter and line with baking parchment. (6-9) (9-12) In a large mixing bowl, mix together the cornmeal, flours, sugar, bicarbonate of soda and salt. Heat the butter in a saucepan over a low heat until melted, then remove from the heat. In another bowl, lightly beat the eggs together with a whisk. Add the melted butter, yogurt, apricots and 240ml/8fl oz/ scant 1 cup water and mix well.

2 Add the egg mixture to the flour mixture and beat slowly with a wooden spoon until just combined, but take care not to overmix. Pour the mixture into the loaf tin and level the surface, using a clean knife. Bake for 1 hour until lightly browned and a skewer inserted into the centre comes out clean. Remove from the oven and leave to cool for 15 minutes, then turn out of the tin, transfer to a wire rack, remove the baking parchment and leave to cool. Serve warm.

(6-9) BAKED APRICOT PURÉE
Put 2 tablespoons of the apricots, 1 tablespoon of the rice flour and 5 tablespoons water in a greased ramekin and mix well. Bake as above for 15 minutes until the apricots are completely soft and the top has lightly browned. Transfer to a blender and add 3 tablespoons water. Blend for 30 seconds, adding extra water 1 teaspoon at a time, until smooth. Serve warm.

(9-12) CORNMEAL APRICOT BAKE
Put 2 tablespoons of the apricots, 1 tablespoon each of the rice flour and cornmeal, 2 tablespoons of the yogurt and 3 tablespoons water in a greased ramekin and mix well. Bake as above for 20 minutes until the apricots are completely soft and the top has lightly browned. Transfer to a blender and pulse for 15 seconds, adding water 1 teaspoon at a time, until the mixture forms a lumpy purée. Serve warm.

This is an old family favourite that my mom used to make when I was growing up. It is loaded with plums and heavy with oats – perfect for breakfast or snacking. My brother David and I loved it when we were little, and now it is a favourite with Nicholas.

Plum Oatmeal Bread

MAKES: 1 loaf (about 16 slices)
PREPARATION TIME: 20 minutes
COOKING TIME: 1 hour
STORAGE: Store in an airtight container for up to 2 days, then refrigerate for up to 3 days or slice and freeze for up to 3 months.

....

unsalted butter, for greasing
120g/4¼oz/1 cup wholemeal spelt flour or wholemeal plain flour
120g/4¼oz/1 cup white spelt flour or white plain flour
100g/3½oz/1 cup porridge oats
140g/5oz/scant ¾ cup cane sugar
1 tbsp baking powder
1 tsp fine sea salt
2 large eggs
240ml/8fl oz/scant 1 cup oat milk, rice milk or water
4 tbsp sunflower oil
2 tsp vanilla extract
280g/10oz plums, pitted and chopped

1 Preheat the oven to 180°C/350°F/gas 4. Grease a 23 x 13cm/9 x 5in loaf tin with butter, line with baking parchment and grease again.

2 (9-12) In a large mixing bowl, mix together the flours, oats, sugar, baking powder and salt. In another bowl, lightly beat the eggs together with a whisk. Add the oat milk, oil and vanilla extract and whisk. Add the egg mixture to the flour mixture and beat slowly with a wooden spoon until just combined, but take care not to overmix. (6-9) Using a large metal spoon, carefully fold in the plums. Pour the mixture into the loaf tin and level the surface, using a clean knife.

3 Bake for 50 minutes–1 hour until lightly browned and a skewer inserted into the centre comes out clean. Remove from the oven and leave to cool for 20 minutes. Run a knife around the edge of the loaf, then turn out of the tin, transfer to a wire rack, remove the baking parchment and leave to cool. Serve warm or at room temperature.

(6-9) **PLUM PURÉE**
Put 4 tablespoons of the plums and 2 tablespoons water in a blender. Blend for 30 seconds, adding extra water 1 teaspoon at a time, until smooth. Serve warm or at room temperature.

(9-12) **PLUM PUDDING**
Put 4 tablespoons of the oats, 2 tablespoons of the plums and 185ml/6fl oz/¾ cup water in a small baking dish. Leave to soak, covered, for 7 hours or overnight at room temperature. Bake as above for 30 minutes until completely soft. Transfer to a blender and add 2 tablespoons water. Pulse for 15 seconds, adding extra water 1 teaspoon at a time, until the mixture forms a lumpy purée. Serve warm.

These are quick to prepare – much easier than cookies. Serve them mid-morning when your kids are home on the weekends, in their lunchbox at school or when they come in from playing.

Cinnamon Raisin Bars

MAKES: 12
PREPARATION TIME: 15 minutes
COOKING TIME: 45 minutes
STORAGE: Store in an airtight container for up to 2 days, then refrigerate for up to 3 days.

....

3 large eggs
240ml/8fl oz/scant 1 cup sunflower oil, plus extra for greasing
240ml/8fl oz/scant 1 cup rice malt syrup or 165g/5¾oz/¾ cup + 2 tbsp cane sugar
2 tsp vanilla extract
300g/10½oz/3 cups porridge oats
180g/6¼oz/1½ cups wholemeal spelt flour or wholemeal plain flour
150g/5½oz/scant 1¼ cups raisins
4 tsp ground cinnamon
1 tsp baking powder
1 tsp fine sea salt

1 Preheat the oven to 170°C/325°F/gas 3 and grease a 23 x 33cm/9 x 13in baking dish with oil. In a bowl, lightly beat the eggs together with a whisk. Mix in the oil, rice malt syrup, vanilla extract and 60ml/2fl oz/¼ cup water (or 120ml/4fl oz/½ cup water if using cane sugar).

2 (6-9) (9-12) In a large mixing bowl, mix together the oats, flour, raisins, cinnamon, baking powder and salt. Add the egg mixture to the flour mixture and stir well with a wooden spoon until mixed. Pour the mixture into the baking dish and smooth the surface with a spatula.

3 Bake for 45 minutes until lightly browned. Remove from oven and leave to cool for 5 minutes. Cut into squares and serve warm or at room temperature.

(6-9)

BAKED OATS PURÉE
Put 4 tablespoons of the oats and 185ml/6fl oz/ ¾ cup water in a small baking dish and mix. Leave to soak, covered, for 7 hours or overnight at room temperature. Bake as above for 30 minutes until completely soft. Transfer to a blender and add 2 tablespoons water. Blend for 30 seconds, adding extra water 1 teaspoon at a time, until smooth. Serve warm.

(9-12)

RAISIN PUDDING
Put 4 tablespoons of the oats, 1 tablespoon of the raisins and 185ml/6fl oz/¾ cup water in a small baking dish and mix. Leave to soak, covered, for 7 hours or overnight at room temperature. Bake as above for 30 minutes until completely soft. Transfer to a blender and add 2 tablespoons water. Pulse for 15 seconds, adding extra water 1 teaspoon at a time, until the mixture forms a lumpy purée. Serve warm.

Most children – and mine – adore berries. I make these muffins with mashed raspberries and chopped peaches – and they can't resist them. Perfect for breakfast or as a snack, these are great for the whole family. Jessica's friend, Josie, couldn't wait to try one!

Peach & Raspberry Muffins

MAKES: 12
PREPARATION TIME: 25 minutes
COOKING TIME: 30 minutes
STORAGE: Refrigerate for up to 3 days.

....

70g/2½oz unsalted butter, plus extra for greasing if needed
240g/8½oz/2 cups wholemeal spelt flour or wholemeal plain flour
100g/3½oz/½ cup cane sugar
2 tsp baking powder
½ tsp fine sea salt
2 large eggs
230ml/7¾fl oz/scant 1 cup oat milk, rice milk or water
125g/4½oz peaches, pitted and diced
80g/2¾oz/scant ⅔ cup fresh or defrosted, frozen raspberries, mashed

1 Preheat the oven to 190°C/375°F/gas 5 and grease a 12-cup muffin tin with butter or line with paper cupcake liners. Heat the butter in a saucepan over a low heat until melted. Remove from the heat and leave to cool slightly. In a bowl, mix together the flour, sugar, baking powder and salt. In a large mixing bowl, lightly beat the eggs together with a whisk. Add the melted butter and oat milk and whisk. Add the flour mixture and whisk until just combined, but take care not to overmix.

2 (6-9) (9-12) Using a large metal spoon, carefully fold in the peaches and raspberries. Spoon the mixture evenly into the muffin cups, filling each cup until it is nearly full. Bake for 25–30 minutes until golden and a skewer inserted into the centre comes out clean. Remove from the oven and leave to cool for 5 minutes, then turn out of the tin and transfer to a wire rack. Serve warm.

(6-9) **PEACH PURÉE**
Put 5 tablespoons of the peaches and 2 tablespoons water in a blender. Blend for 30 seconds, adding extra water 1 teaspoon at a time, until smooth. Serve warm or at room temperature.

(9-12) **PEACH & RASPBERRY MIX**
Put 4 tablespoons of the peaches, 1 tablespoon of the raspberries and 2 tablespoons water in a blender. Pulse for 15 seconds, adding extra water 1 teaspoon at a time, until the mixture forms a lumpy purée. Serve warm or at room temperature.

Irresistible to children and grown-ups, these are densely chocolatey and lightly sweet. These brownies are made with sweet potato so they are a twist on the American classic. Although the rice malt syrup won't over-excite you, the chocolate will, so go easy.

Sweet Potato Brownies

MAKES: 9
PREPARATION TIME: 30 minutes
COOKING TIME: 40 minutes
STORAGE: Refrigerate for up to 3 days.

....

350g/12oz sweet potatoes, peeled and diced

90g/3¼oz unsalted butter, plus extra for greasing

40g/1½oz/½ cup unsweetened cocoa powder

2 tsp vanilla extract

2 large eggs

240ml/8fl oz/scant 1 cup rice malt syrup or 140g/5oz/scant ¾ cup cane sugar

135g/4¾oz/1 cup + 1 tbsp wholemeal spelt flour or wholemeal plain flour

1½ tsp baking powder

½ tsp fine sea salt

1 Preheat the oven to 180°C/350°F/gas 4. Grease a 20 x 20cm/8 x 8in baking tin with butter, line with baking parchment and grease again. Put the sweet potatoes in a steamer and steam, covered, for 8–10 minutes until completely soft. **6-9** **9-12** Transfer to a large bowl and mash thoroughly until smooth.

2 Heat the butter in a saucepan over a low heat until melted. Remove from the heat, add the cocoa powder and vanilla extract and stir until well combined. In a small bowl, lightly beat the eggs together with a whisk. Add the eggs, cocoa mixture and rice malt syrup to the sweet potatoes and mix well. In another bowl, mix together the flour, baking powder and salt, then add to the sweet potato mixture and fold until well mixed, but take care not to overmix.

3 Spoon the mixture into the baking tin and smooth the surface with a spatula. Bake for 35–40 minutes until the surface is cracked and a skewer inserted into the centre comes out clean. Remove from the oven and leave to cool in the tin for 5 minutes. Cut into squares and transfer to a wire rack to cool. Serve warm or at room temperature.

 SWEET POTATO PURÉE
Put 5 tablespoons of the steamed sweet potato and 3 tablespoons water in a blender. Blend for 30 seconds, adding extra water 1 teaspoon at a time, until smooth. Serve warm.

 BUTTERY SWEET POTATO MASH
Put 5 tablespoons of the steamed sweet potato and 3 tablespoons water in a blender. Pulse for 15 seconds, adding extra water 1 teaspoon at a time, until the mixture forms a lumpy purée. Mix in 1 teaspoon of the melted butter and serve warm.

It's hard to go wrong with lemon desserts, and after a satisfying meal, this pudding is perfect because it is light and refreshing. The drizzled mango accents the flavour beautifully and is wonderful for your baby.

Lemon Upside-Down Cake with Mango Purée

SERVES: 10
PREPARATION TIME: 20 minutes
COOKING TIME: 45 minutes
STORAGE: Refrigerate the cake and the mango purée for up to 3 days.

....

75g/2½oz/⅓ cup soft brown sugar
180g/6¼oz unsalted butter, softened, plus extra for greasing
2 lemons, finely sliced and seeds removed
185g/6½oz/heaped 1½ cups wholemeal spelt flour or wholemeal plain flour
2 tsp baking powder
55g/2oz/heaped ⅓ cup fast-cook polenta
½ tsp fine sea salt
110g/3¾oz/heaped ½ cup cane sugar
2 large eggs
1 tsp vanilla extract
zest of 1 lemon
125ml/4fl oz/½ cup oat milk, rice milk or water

FOR THE MANGO PURÉE
2 mangoes, peeled, pitted and chopped

1 Preheat the oven to 180°C/350°F/gas 4 and grease a 20cm/8in cake tin with butter. Put the brown sugar and 60g/2¼oz of the butter in a saucepan and heat over a low heat for 2–3 minutes, stirring continuously, until the butter has melted and the brown sugar has dissolved. Pour the mixture into the cake tin and arrange the lemons over the top (as close together as you can). Mix the flour, baking powder, polenta and salt in a large mixing bowl.

2 Using an electric mixer, beat together the cane sugar and the remaining butter in a mixing bowl for 3 minutes until creamy. Beat in the eggs, one at a time, for 30 seconds each until thoroughly incorporated, then beat in the vanilla extract and lemon zest. (9-12) Gradually beat in the flour mixture and the oat milk, alternating. Beat until well combined, but take care not to overmix.

3 Pour the mixture over the lemons and smooth the surface with a spatula. Bake for 35–40 minutes until lightly browned and a skewer inserted into the centre comes out clean. Remove from the oven and leave to cool for 20 minutes, then turn out of the tin, transfer to a wire rack and leave to cool.

4 Meanwhile, make the purée. Put the mango in a blender and blend for 1 minute, adding water 1 tablespoon at a time, until smooth. (6-9) Serve the cake warm, drizzled with the purée.

(6-9) MANGO PURÉE
Put 5 tablespoons of the mango purée in a bowl and serve warm or at room temperature.

(9-12) CHUNKY MANGO PUDDING
Put 5 tablespoons of the mango chunks and 1 tablespoon of the oat milk in a blender. Pulse for 15 seconds, adding water 1 teaspoon at a time, until the mixture forms a lumpy purée. Serve warm or at room temperature.

This cake, which is very easy to make, is also very rich and should be enjoyed in thin slices – if you can resist the urge to go for more. It is almost like baked mousse, although the pear lightens it and adds texture.

Chocolate Pear Cake

MAKES: 1 cake
PREPARATION TIME: 25 minutes
COOKING TIME: 20 minutes
STORAGE: Store in an airtight container for up to 2 days, then refrigerate for up to 3 days or freeze for up to 3 months.

....

250g/9oz unsalted butter, softened, plus extra for greasing
100g/3½oz dark chocolate, 70% cocoa solids, broken into small pieces
4 large eggs
125g/4½oz/heaped ⅔ cup cane sugar
4 tbsp natural yogurt
50g/1¾oz/scant ½ cup wholemeal spelt flour or wholemeal plain flour
1 pear, cored and finely chopped

1 Preheat the oven to 180°C/350°F/gas 4 and grease a 20cm/8in cake tin with butter. Put the butter and chocolate in a large heatproof bowl and rest it over a pan of gently simmering water, making sure that the bottom of the bowl does not touch the water. Stir occasionally until the butter and chocolate have melted. Put the eggs and sugar in a bowl and beat, using an electric mixer, for 10 minutes until pale and fluffy. (9-12) Mix the yogurt into the chocolate mixture to cool it a little, then add the chocolate mixture to the egg mixture and mix well. Add the flour and fold until well mixed, but take care not to overmix.

2 Pour the mixture into the cake tin. Spoon the pear into the tin, then push it down under the surface of the mixture with the back of the spoon. Bake for 15–20 minutes until firm to the touch and a skewer inserted into the centre of the cake comes out clean. Remove from the oven and leave to cool for 15 minutes, then turn out of the tin, transfer to a wire rack and leave to cool. Serve warm or at room temperature.

(6-9)

PEAR PURÉE
Put ½ of the pear and 2 tablespoons water in a blender. Blend for 30 seconds, adding extra water 1 teaspoon at a time, until smooth. Serve warm or at room temperature.

(9-12)

PEAR & YOGURT
Put ½ of the pear, 2 tablespoons of the yogurt and 1 tablespoon water in a blender. Pulse for 15 seconds, adding extra water 1 teaspoon at a time, until the mixture forms a lumpy purée. Serve warm or at room temperature.

Beautifully spiced and sweet, here's a dessert with no added sugar. The pecans on top become crunchy and provide a nice contrast to the soft, warm fruit. I made this for a girlie Sunday lunch and there wasn't a crumb left in the dish.

Baked Spiced Fruit

SERVES: 2 adults, 1 child and 1 baby
PREPARATION TIME: 25 minutes
COOKING TIME: 45 minutes
STORAGE: Refrigerate for up to 3 days.

. . . .

225g/8oz peaches, pitted and chopped
1 pear, cored and chopped
85g/3oz/scant ½ cup dried unsulphured apricots, chopped
225g/8oz pineapple, peeled, cored and chopped
230ml/7¾fl oz/scant 1 cup peach juice, apricot juice or pineapple juice
2 tbsp lemon juice
2 tbsp wholemeal spelt flour or wholemeal plain flour
1 tsp ground cinnamon
¼ tsp ground cloves
100g/3½oz/1 cup pecans, halved
natural yogurt, to serve

1 Preheat the oven to 180°C/350°F/gas 4. Put the peaches, pear and apricots in a 20 x 20cm/8 x 8in baking dish and mix well. Stir in the pineapple and set aside.

2 Pour the peach juice and lemon juice into a saucepan. Add the flour, cinnamon and cloves and mix together. Bring to the boil over a high heat, stirring continuously. Cook for 3–4 minutes, stirring frequently, until the sauce has thickened, then pour over the fruit. Sprinkle the pecans evenly over the top and bake for 40 minutes until the fruit is bubbling and the pecans have browned. Remove from the oven and leave to cool in the baking dish for 5 minutes. Serve warm or at room temperature with yogurt.

(6-9) BAKED PEACH, PEAR & APRICOT PURÉE
Put 4 tablespoons of the peach, pear and apricot mixture and 1 tablespoon of the peach juice in a ramekin. Bake as above for 15 minutes until the fruit is completely soft. Transfer to a blender and blend for 30 seconds, adding water 1 teaspoon at a time, until smooth. Serve warm.

(9-12) BAKED FRUIT WITH YOGURT
Put 4 tablespoons of the peach, pear and apricot mixture and 1 tablespoon of the peach juice in a ramekin. Bake as above for 15 minutes until the fruit is completely soft. Transfer to a blender and add 2 tablespoons of yogurt. Pulse for 15 seconds, adding water 1 teaspoon at a time, until the mixture forms a lumpy purée. Serve warm.

Peach & Blueberry Pie

SERVES: 8
PREPARATION TIME: 45 minutes,
plus 30 minutes chilling
COOKING TIME: 50 minutes
STORAGE: Refrigerate for up to 3 days.

....

FOR THE PASTRY

240g/8½oz/2 cups wholemeal spelt
flour or wholemeal plain flour,
plus extra for dusting
½ tsp fine sea salt
125g/4½oz chilled unsalted butter,
diced

FOR THE FILLING

30g/1oz/¼ cup wholemeal spelt flour
or wholemeal plain flour
1 tbsp cornflour, ground arrowroot
or kuzu
80ml/2½fl oz/⅓ cup rice malt syrup
or 55g/2oz/heaped ¼ cup cane sugar
½ tsp ground nutmeg
¼ tsp fine sea salt
1 tbsp lemon juice
1 tsp lemon zest
450g/1lb/scant 3 cups blueberries
2 peaches, pitted and diced

1 To make the pastry, mix the flour and salt in a bowl and rub in the butter with your fingertips until the mixture resembles breadcrumbs. Add 4–6 tablespoons cold water, 1 tablespoon at a time, and mix with a fork until it comes together to form a dough. Shape ⅔ of the pastry into a ball and the remaining dough into a smaller ball, then wrap each ball in cling film and chill in the fridge for 30 minutes.

2 Dust a piece of baking parchment with flour. Take ⅔ of the pastry and roll out into a circle about 32cm/12½in in diameter and trim around the edges, using a sharp knife, to neaten. Put a 25cm/10in pie dish, face-down, on top of the pastry, then, holding the baking parchment and pie dish together, turn them over to drop the pastry into the dish. Ease the pastry into place, pressing down gently to remove any air pockets. Neaten the edge using a sharp knife.

3 To make the filling, put the flour, cornflour, rice malt syrup, nutmeg, salt, lemon juice and lemon zest in a bowl and mix until combined.   Add the blueberries and peaches and mix well. Pour the filling into the pastry-lined pie dish and level the surface with a spatula.

4 Preheat the oven to 230°C/450°F/gas 8. Dust another piece of baking parchment with flour, take the remaining pastry and roll out into a circle about 27cm/10¾in in diameter and trim around the edges, using a sharp knife, to neaten. Ease the pastry onto the top of the pie and press down around the rim with your fingers to seal and crimp the edge. Using a sharp knife, cut a small cross in the centre of the pastry lid.

5 Bake for 10 minutes, then turn the heat down to 180°C/350°F/gas 4 and bake for another 35–40 minutes until the crust is lightly browned and the juices are bubbling through the air hole. Remove from the oven and leave to cool in the pie dish for 5 minutes. Serve warm or at room temperature.

 BAKED PEACH PURÉE
Put 5 tablespoons of the peaches and 1 tablespoon water in a ramekin. Bake as above for 15 minutes until the peaches are completely soft. Transfer to a blender and blend for 30 seconds, adding water 1 teaspoon at a time, until smooth. Serve warm.

 BAKED PEACHES & BLUEBERRIES
Put 3 tablespoons each of the peaches and blueberries and 1 tablespoon water in ramekin. Bake as above for 15 minutes until the fruit is completely soft. Transfer to a blender and pulse for 15 seconds, adding water 1 teaspoon at a time, until the mixture forms a lumpy purée. Serve warm.

Here is a gorgeous tart. Bake it when plums and blackberries are at their peak in the summer. You can use other fruits, such as peaches, nectarines, cherries, strawberries or blueberries. I often let the children bake mini versions of this alongside the big one – just bake them for less time.

Plum & Blackberry Tart

SERVES: 10
PREPARATION TIME: 35 minutes, plus 30 minutes chilling
COOKING TIME: 40 minutes
STORAGE: Refrigerate for up to 3 days.

....

FOR THE PASTRY
240g/8½oz/2 cups wholemeal spelt flour or wholemeal plain flour, plus extra for dusting
70g/2½oz/heaped ⅓ cup cane sugar
1½ tsp fine sea salt
125g/4½oz chilled unsalted butter, diced

FOR THE FILLING
4 tbsp wholemeal spelt flour or wholemeal plain flour
1 tbsp cornflour, ground arrowroot or kuzu
900g/2lb plums, pitted and chopped
200g/7oz/scant 1 cup blackberries
80ml/2½fl oz/⅓ cup rice malt syrup or 55g/2oz/heaped ¼ cup cane sugar
2 tbsp lemon juice
natural yogurt, to serve

1 Grease a 30cm/12in shallow, fluted tart tin with oil. To make the pastry, mix the flour, sugar and salt in a large mixing bowl and rub in the butter with your fingertips until the mixture resembles breadcrumbs. Add 2–3 tablespoons cold water, 1 tablespoon at a time, and mix with a fork until it comes together to form a dough. Shape the pastry into a ball, wrap in cling film and chill in the fridge for 30 minutes.

2 Dust a piece of baking parchment with flour and roll out the pastry into a circle about 35cm/14in in diameter and trim around the edges, using a sharp knife, to neaten. Put the tin, face-down, on top of the pastry, then, holding the baking parchment and tin together, turn them over to drop the pastry into the tin. Ease the pastry into place, pressing down gently to remove any air pockets. Neaten the edge using a sharp knife.

3 Preheat the oven to 180°C/350°F/gas 4. To make the filling, mix together the flour and cornflour in a large bowl. (6-9) (9-12) Add the plums, blackberries, rice malt syrup and lemon juice and mix well. Spoon the mixture over the pastry and smooth the surface with a spatula.

4 Bake for 40 minutes until the top is bubbling. Remove from the oven and leave to cool for 5 minutes, then turn out of the tin, transfer to a wire rack and leave to cool. Serve warm or at room temperature with yogurt.

(6-9)

BAKED PLUM PURÉE
Put 5 tablespoons of the plums and 1 tablespoon water in a ramekin and bake as above for 15 minutes until completely soft. Transfer to a blender and blend for 30 seconds, adding water 1 teaspoon at a time, until smooth. Serve warm.

(9-12)

BAKED PLUMS & BLACKBERRIES
Put 3 tablespoons each of the plums and blackberries and 1 tablespoon water in a ramekin and bake as above for 15 minutes until completely soft. Transfer to a blender and pulse for 15 seconds, adding water 1 teaspoon at a time, until the mixture forms a lumpy purée. Serve warm.

It's easier than you think pitting cherries, and this dessert is so delicious that it's worth the effort (just make sure you buy a cherry stoner to help you). If you don't have the time, though, you can use frozen or tinned, unsweetened cherries instead.

Cherry Crumbles

MAKES: 4
PREPARATION TIME: 30 minutes
COOKING TIME: 30 minutes
STORAGE: Refrigerate for up to 3 days.

....

FOR THE TOPPING
55g/2oz/heaped ¼ cup cane sugar
60g/2¼oz/½ cup wholemeal
    spelt flour or wholemeal plain flour
½ tsp fine sea salt
3 tbsp sunflower oil, plus extra for
    greasing
natural yogurt, to serve

FOR THE FILLING
2 tbsp cornflour, ground arrowroot
    or kuzu
500g/1lb 2oz fresh, stoned cherries
    or frozen or tinned pitted cherries
2 tsp lemon juice
1 tsp lemon zest
½ tsp vanilla extract

1 Preheat the oven to 190°C/375°F/gas 5 and grease 4 x 200–250ml/ 7–9fl oz/scant 1 cup–1 cup ramekins with oil. To make the filling, put the cornflour and 3 tablespoons cold water in a bowl and mix together to make a smooth paste. Add the cherries, lemon juice, lemon zest and vanilla extract and stir until mixed well. Spoon the mixture evenly into the ramekins.

2 In another bowl, mix together the sugar, flour, salt and oil until just combined and the mixture resembles coarse breadcrumbs. Spoon the mixture evenly over the cherries. Bake for 25–30 minutes until bubbling and lightly browned. Remove from the oven and leave to cool for 5 minutes. Serve warm with yogurt.

(6-9) CHERRY PURÉE
Put 5 tablespoons of the cherries and 2 tablespoons water in a blender. Blend for 30 seconds, adding extra water 1 teaspoon at a time, until smooth. Serve warm or at room temperature.

(9-12) BAKED CHERRIES WITH YOGURT
Put 4 tablespoons of the cherries and 2 tablespoons water in a ramekin and bake as above for 15 minutes until completely soft. Transfer to a blender and add 2 tablespoons of yogurt. Pulse for 15 seconds, adding water 1 teaspoon at a time, until the mixture forms a lumpy purée. Serve warm.

One of my favourites. It's so good that it's hard to resist at any time of day and I find myself wanting it for breakfast. My friend Jazz says her son Jonah talks about the wonders of my crumble, and my friend Julie loves it.

Rhubarb Raspberry Crumble

SERVES: 2 adults, 1 child and 1 baby
PREPARATION TIME: 20 minutes
COOKING TIME: 1 hour
STORAGE: Store in an airtight container for up to 2 days, then refrigerate for up to 3 days.

. . . .

450g/1lb fresh or defrosted, frozen rhubarb, chopped
300g/10½oz/scant 2½ cups fresh or defrosted, frozen raspberries
165g/5¾oz/¾ cup + 1 tbsp cane sugar
natural yogurt, to serve

FOR THE CRUMBLE
200g/7oz/heaped 1⅔ cups wholemeal spelt flour or wholemeal plain flour
75g/2½oz/¾ cup porridge oats
25g/1oz/¼ cup buckwheat flakes
110g/3¾oz/heaped ½ cup cane sugar
1½ tsp ground cinnamon
½ tsp fine sea salt
125g/4½oz unsalted butter or sunflower oil, plus extra for greasing

1 Preheat the oven to 170°C/325°F/gas 3 and grease a 23 x 23cm/ 9 x 9in baking tin with butter. To make the crumble, put the flour, oats, buckwheat flakes, sugar, cinnamon and salt in a large mixing bowl and mix well. Heat the butter in a saucepan over a low heat until melted, then remove from the heat. Add the melted butter to the flour mixture and stir until the mixture resembles coarse breadcrumbs. Spread ⅔ of the crumble mixture over the bottom of the baking tin, pressing down firmly with the back of a metal spoon. Leave the remaining crumble to one side.

2 In another bowl, mix together the rhubarb, raspberries and sugar. Pour the fruit mixture on top of the crumble mixture in the baking tin, then evenly sprinkle the remaining crumble mixture over the top. Bake for 50–60 minutes until lightly browned. Serve warm or cold with yogurt.

(6-9) OAT & BUCKWHEAT PORRIDGE PURÉE
Put 2 tablespoons each of the oats and buckwheat flakes, 1 teaspoon of yogurt and 185ml/6fl oz/¾ cup water in a saucepan. Leave to soak, covered, for 7 hours or overnight at room temperature. Bring to a simmer over high heat, then turn the heat down to low and cook, stirring occasionally, for 10 minutes until completely soft. Transfer to a blender and add 2 tablespoons water. Blend for 30 seconds, adding extra water 1 teaspoon at a time, until smooth. Serve warm.

 OAT, BUCKWHEAT, RHUBARB & RASPBERRY PORRIDGE
Put 6 rhubarb pieces, 2 tablespoons each of the oats and buckwheat flakes, 1 teaspoon of yogurt and 185ml/6 fl oz/¾ cup water in a saucepan. Leave to soak, covered, for 7 hours or overnight at room temperature. Bring to a simmer over a high heat, then turn the heat down to low and cook, stirring occasionally, for 10 minutes until completely soft. Transfer to a blender and add 1 tablespoon of the raspberries and 2 tablespoons water. Pulse for 15 seconds, adding extra water 1 teaspoon at a time, until the mixture forms a lumpy purée. Serve warm.

Sometimes it's nice to have the delight of a pie – without the bother of the pastry. My sister Jan says her kids prefer this version to hers, even though mine uses a lot less sugar.

Apple Bake with Walnut Topping

SERVES: 8
PREPARATION TIME: 25 minutes
COOKING TIME: 1 hour
STORAGE: Store in an airtight container for up to 2 days, then refrigerate for up to 3 days.

....

FOR THE FILLING
3 tbsp wholemeal spelt flour or
  wholemeal plain flour
55g/2oz/heaped ¼ cup cane sugar
1 tsp ground cinnamon
¼ tsp ground nutmeg
½ tsp fine sea salt
600g/1lb 5oz sweet apples,
  cored and chopped
1 tbsp lemon juice

FOR THE TOPPING
50g/1¾oz/scant ½ cup wholemeal spelt
  flour or wholemeal plain flour
35g/1¼oz/⅓ cup buckwheat flakes
15g/½oz/scant ¼ cup walnuts, roughly
  chopped
25g/1oz/3 tbsp cane sugar
⅛ tsp fine sea salt
40g/1½oz chilled, unsalted butter,
  diced, plus extra for greasing
natural yogurt, to serve

1 Preheat the oven to 180°C/350°F/gas 4 and grease a 25cm/10in pie dish with butter. To make the filling, put the flour, sugar, cinnamon, nutmeg and salt in a large mixing bowl and mix well. **(9-12)** Put the apples in a small bowl and sprinkle the lemon juice over them. Add to the flour mixture and mix well.

2 **(6-9)** To make the topping, put the flour, buckwheat flakes, walnuts, sugar and salt in a small bowl and mix well. Rub in the butter with your fingertips until the mixture resembles breadcrumbs. Put the apple mixture in the pie dish and spoon the topping mixture over the top. Bake for 50–60 minutes until the filling is bubbling and the topping has browned. Serve hot with yogurt.

(6-9) BAKED BUCKWHEAT PURÉE
Put 4 tablespoons of the buckwheat flakes, 1 teaspoon of yogurt and 125ml/4fl oz/½ cup water in a small baking dish. Leave to soak, covered, for 7 hours or overnight at room temperature. Bake as above for 35 minutes until completely soft. Transfer to a blender and add 2 tablespoons water. Blend for 30 seconds, adding extra water 1 teaspoon at a time, until smooth. Serve warm.

(9-12) BAKED BUTTERY APPLE & BUCKWHEAT
Put 4 tablespoons of the buckwheat flakes, 1 teaspoon of yogurt and 125ml/4fl oz/½ cup water in a small baking dish. Leave to soak, covered, for 7 hours or overnight at room temperature. Add 6 apple pieces and 1 teaspoon of the butter and mix well. Bake as above for 35 minutes until the apple is completely soft. Transfer to a blender and add 2 tablespoons water. Pulse for 15 seconds, adding extra water 1 teaspoon at a time, until the mixture forms a lumpy purée. Serve warm.

Loaded with fruit, this is a cross between a tray bake and a pie. Brian and I have this for breakfast with a big blob of yogurt; Jessie and Nicholas take it to school for their snack; and little Cassie likes it anytime.

Apple & Blueberry Bake

SERVES: 2 adults, 1 child and 1 baby
PREPARATION TIME: 20 minutes
COOKING TIME: 50 minutes
STORAGE: Store in an airtight container for up to 2 days, then refrigerate for up to 3 days.

....

300g/10½oz/2 cups fresh or
    defrosted, frozen blueberries
300g/10½oz apples, cored and chopped
1 tbsp lemon juice
1 tbsp cornflour, ground arrowroot
    or kuzu
150g/5½oz/1½ cups porridge oats
50g/1¾oz/½ cup buckwheat flakes
110g/3¾oz/heaped ½ cup cane sugar
1 tsp baking powder
½ tsp fine sea salt
6 tbsp sunflower oil, plus extra for
    greasing
1 tsp vanilla extract

1 Preheat the oven to 180°C/350°F/gas 4 and grease a 19 x 26cm/ 7½ x 10½in baking tin with oil. (6-9) (9-12) In a large bowl, mix the blueberries, apples, lemon juice and cornflour and set aside. In another bowl, mix together the oats, buckwheat flakes, sugar, baking powder and salt. Add the oil, vanilla extract and 150ml/5fl oz/scant ⅔ cup water and mix until well combined.

2 Spread the oat mixture in the bottom of the baking tin and smooth the surface with a spatula. Pour the blueberry mixture over the top and smooth the surface again. Bake for 50 minutes until the top is bubbling. Remove from the oven and leave to cool for 5 minutes. Cut into squares and serve warm or at room temperature.

(6-9) **BAKED APPLE & BUCKWHEAT PURÉE**
Put 6 apple pieces, 4 tablespoons of the buckwheat flakes and 185ml/ 6fl oz/¾ cup water in a bowl and mix. Transfer to a greased ramekin and bake as above for 35 minutes until completely soft. Transfer to a blender and add 2 tablespoons water. Blend for 30 seconds, adding extra water 1 teaspoon at a time, until smooth. Serve warm.

(9-12) **BAKED APPLE & BLUEBERRY**
Put 1½ tablespoons each of the apples and blueberries, 4 tablespoons of the buckwheat flakes and 4 tablespoons water in a bowl and mix. Transfer to a greased ramekin and bake as above for 35 minutes until completely soft. Transfer to a blender and add 2 tablespoons water. Pulse for 15 seconds, adding extra water 1 teaspoon at a time, until the mixture forms a lumpy purée. Serve warm.

Who doesn't love rice pudding? It's a dish you can stick in the oven and let cook to perfection. Gently spiced and with sweet raisins, here is a healthy treat for everyone.

Oven Rice Pudding

SERVES: 2 adults, 1 child and 1 baby
PREPARATION TIME: 20 minutes, plus at least 7 hours soaking
COOKING TIME: 2 hours
STORAGE: Refrigerate for up to 3 days.

....

200g/7oz/1 cup sweet brown rice or short grain brown rice
1 tbsp natural yogurt
2 large eggs
75g/2½oz/⅓ cup + 2 tbsp cane sugar
750ml/26fl oz/3 cups oat milk or rice milk
30g/1oz/¼ cup raisins, chopped
1 tsp vanilla extract
1 tsp ground cinnamon
¼ tsp ground nutmeg
1 tsp fine sea salt

1 Put the rice and yogurt in a deep baking dish and cover generously with warm water. Leave to soak, covered, for 7 hours or overnight at room temperature. **(6-9)** **(9-12)**

2 Preheat the oven to 170°C/325°F/gas 3. Drain and rinse the rice, then return to the baking dish. In a small bowl, lightly beat the eggs together with a whisk. Add the eggs, sugar, oat milk, raisins, vanilla extract, cinnamon, nutmeg and salt to the baking dish and whisk until the sugar has dissolved and the cinnamon and nutmeg have dispersed.

3 Bake for 30 minutes until a brown skin has formed on top of the pudding. Stir in the skin and bake for a further 15 minutes. Stir again and bake for another 1 hour 15 minutes until the rice is completely soft and the top has browned. Serve hot or cold.

(6-9) **SWEET RICE BAKE PURÉE**
Put 2 tablespoons of the soaked rice and 8 tablespoons of the oat milk in a small baking dish and mix. Bake as above for 1 hour 15 minutes until the rice is completely soft. Transfer to a blender and add 2 tablespoons water. Blend for 30 seconds, adding extra water 1 teaspoon at a time, until smooth. Serve warm.

(9-12) **SWEET RICE & RAISIN PUDDING**
Put 2 tablespoons of the soaked rice, 8 tablespoons of the oat milk and 1 teaspoon of the raisins in a small baking dish and mix. Bake as above for 1 hour 15 minutes until the rice is completely soft. Transfer to a blender and add 2 tablespoons water. Pulse for 15 seconds, adding extra water 1 teaspoon at a time, until the mixture forms a lumpy purée. Serve warm.

My husband Brian was dubious when I first created this, because it looks a little strange in the making. But once it was finished, I couldn't keep him away. It has a beautiful colour and the flavours of autumn and Christmas.

Pumpkin Pudding

SERVES: 2 adults, 1 child and 1 baby
PREPARATION TIME: 20 minutes, plus cooling, plus at least 1 hour setting
COOKING TIME: 50 minutes
STORAGE: Refrigerate for up to 3 days.

....

500g/1lb 2oz/2 cups natural yogurt, plus extra to serve (optional)
110g/3¾oz/heaped ½ cup cane sugar
1½ tsp ground cinnamon
½ tsp ground nutmeg
½ tsp ground cloves
½ tsp ground allspice
½ tsp fine sea salt
320g/11¼oz pumpkin, peeled, deseeded and diced or squash, deseeded and diced
80g/2¾oz chilled, unsalted butter, diced

1 Preheat the oven to 180°C/350°F/gas 4. (9-12) In a bowl, mix together the yogurt, sugar, spices and salt. (6-9) Put the pumpkin, butter and spice mixture in a baking dish and mix, making sure the pumpkin is covered in the spice mixture.

2 Bake, covered, for 50 minutes until soft. Remove from the oven and leave to cool completely. Transfer the mixture to a blender and blend for 1 minute until smooth. Spoon the mixture into serving dishes. Cover with cling film and leave to set in the fridge for at least 1 hour. Serve cold with extra yogurt, if you like.

 BAKED PUMPKIN PURÉE
Put 5 tablespoons of the pumpkin and 1 tablespoon water in a ramekin. Bake as above for 30 minutes until the pumpkin is completely soft. Transfer to a blender and add 3 tablespoons water. Blend for 30 seconds, adding extra water 1 teaspoon at a time, until smooth. Serve warm.

(9-12) **BAKED PUMPKIN WITH YOGURT**
Put 5 tablespoons of the pumpkin, 1 tablespoon water and 1 teaspoon of the butter in a ramekin. Bake as above for 30 minutes until the pumpkin is completely soft. Transfer to a blender and add 2 tablespoons of the yogurt and 2 tablespoons water. Pulse for 15 seconds, adding extra water 1 teaspoon at a time, until the mixture forms a lumpy purée. Serve warm.

I grew up on baked squash and love the smell of cinnamon and melting butter that wafts from the oven while it bakes. This version, with the apple and chopped pecans, is delightful.

Cinnamon Acorn Squash

SERVES: 2 adults, 1 child and 1 baby
PREPARATION TIME: 15 minutes
COOKING TIME: 50 minutes
STORAGE: Refrigerate for up to 3 days.

....

extra virgin olive oil, for greasing
2 acorn squash, halved and deseeded
2 apples, cored and chopped
30g/1oz/generous ¼ cup pecans, chopped
2 tsp rice malt syrup or 1 tsp cane sugar
¼ tsp ground cinnamon
15g/½oz unsalted butter

1 Preheat the oven to 180°C/350°F/gas 4 and grease a large baking dish with oil. Put the squash halves flesh-side down in the baking dish and bake for 30 minutes until softening. Remove from the oven and turn the squash halves skin-side down in the baking dish.

2 Put the apples, pecans, rice malt syrup and cinnamon in a bowl and mix well. Spoon the apple mixture into each squash half until filled to the top. Divide the butter into 4 pieces and put 1 piece on top of each squash half. Bake for 20 minutes until the squash and apples are soft. Serve hot.

 SQUASH & APPLE BAKE PURÉE
Put ½ of 1 squash skin-side down in a greased baking dish and fill with 2 tablespoons of the apple. Bake as above for 25 minutes until the squash and apple are completely soft. Transfer to a blender and blend for 30 seconds, adding water 1 teaspoon at a time, until smooth. Serve warm.

 BUTTERY SQUASH & APPLE BAKE
Put ½ of 1 squash skin-side down in a greased baking dish and fill with 2 tablespoons of the apple and 1 teaspoon of the butter. Bake as above for 25 minutes until the squash and apple are completely soft. Transfer to a blender and pulse for 15 seconds, adding water 1 teaspoon at a time, until the mixture forms a lumpy purée. Serve warm.

An interesting marriage of fruit and root, this has
a lovely sweetness. The combination of fruit and
vegetable provides a great mix of nutrients as well,
and it's a quick dish to prepare.

Banana & Sweet Potato Pudding

SERVES: 2 adults, 1 child and 1 baby
PREPARATION TIME: 20 minutes
COOKING TIME: 1 hour
STORAGE: Refrigerate for up to 3 days.

....

unsalted butter, for greasing
225g/8oz sweet potato, diced
240g/8½oz/2 cups wholemeal
    spelt flour or wholemeal plain flour
110g/3¾oz/heaped ½ cup cane sugar
1 tsp ground cinnamon
¼ tsp ground nutmeg
½ tsp fine sea salt
1 large egg
185ml/6fl oz/¾ cup oat milk or
    rice milk
8 tbsp sunflower oil
1½ tsp vanilla extract
2 bananas, quartered lengthways
    and chopped
natural yogurt, to serve

1 Preheat the oven to 180°C/350°F/gas 4 and grease a baking dish
with butter. Put the sweet potato in a steamer and steam, covered,
for 15 minutes until completely soft. Transfer to a bowl and mash
thoroughly until smooth. **(6-9)** **(9-12)**

2 In a large mixing bowl, mix together the flour, sugar, cinnamon,
nutmeg and salt. In another bowl, lightly beat the egg with a whisk, then
add the oat milk, oil, vanilla extract, bananas and mashed sweet potato
and mix. Add the egg mixture to the flour mixture and stir until combined.
Pour the mixture into the baking dish and bake for 45 minutes until lightly
browned and set. Remove from the oven and leave to cool for 5 minutes.
Serve hot with yogurt.

(6-9) BAKED BANANA & SWEET POTATO PURÉE
Put 6 banana pieces in a bowl and mash well. Add 3 tablespoons of the
mashed sweet potato and 1 tablespoon water and mix well. Transfer to a
greased ramekin and bake as above for 20 minutes until lightly browned
and set. Remove from the oven and leave to cool slightly. Transfer to a
blender and add 1 tablespoon water. Blend for 30 seconds, adding extra
water 1 teaspoon at a time, until smooth. Serve warm.

(9-12) BAKED BANANA & SWEET POTATO
Put 6 banana pieces in a bowl and mash well. Add 3 tablespoons of the
mashed sweet potato, 1 teaspoon of the oil and 1 tablespoon water and mix
well. Transfer to a greased ramekin and bake as above for 20 minutes until
lightly browned and set. Remove from the oven and leave to cool slightly.
Transfer to a blender and add 1 tablespoon water. Pulse for 15 seconds,
adding extra water 1 teaspoon at a time, until the mixture forms a lumpy
purée. Serve warm.

Index